# EXPLORING THE PACIFIC WONDERS: NATIONAL PARKS OF THE PACIFIC REGION

A Comprehensive Travel Guide to California, Oregon, Washington, and Hawaii's Natural Treasures

EVERETT WILDER

*"To the adventurers, the wanderers, and the dreamers who find their spirit renewed in the quiet of towering forests, the roar of waterfalls, and the expanse of open skies. May you always find your way back to nature's embrace."*

# Contents

# Introduction

EXPLORING THE PACIFIC'S NATURAL TREASURES

Welcome to the heart of the Pacific region, where towering redwoods, volcanic peaks, coastal rainforests, and desert landscapes converge to create some of the most breathtaking national parks in the world. This book is your guide to exploring the natural wonders of California, Oregon, Washington, and Hawaii— each state offering its own unique blend of geological marvels, diverse ecosystems, and rich cultural histories.

## The Goal of This Book

The Pacific region's national parks are more than stunning backdrops; they are living, breathing museums of nature's artistry and history. This guide, the first of seven books in this series, aims to take you on an immersive journey through these magnificent landscapes, unveiling their most iconic landmarks, hidden gems, and outdoor adventures.

To comprehensively explore America's national parks, I'm breaking the country into seven distinct quadrants, each representing a unique section of the nation's diverse natural beauty. In this first installment, we'll delve into the breathtaking parks of the Pacific region, rich with towering redwoods, active volcanoes, and dramatic coastlines. Alongside exploring these natural wonders, we'll also delve into the intriguing mysteries and sightings surrounding these parks, adding an element of fun and intrigue to our journey. Each subsequent book will invite you to discover the treasures of the other quadrants, from the majestic peaks of the Rockies to the serene beauty of the East Coast's lush forests.

My deep love for national parks drives this project. I hope to help you appreciate their beauty and experience the profound mental health benefits of exploring these treasured lands. Whether you're a seasoned explorer, a casual hiker, or someone who dreams of wandering through pristine wilderness, this book is designed to inspire and inform, helping you make the most of your visit.

By the end of this journey, you'll gain a deeper appreciation for these natural wonders and a better understanding of their history and significance. From the granite cliffs of Yosemite to the lava flows of Hawai'i Volcanoes, each chapter dives into the unique stories, geological formations, and conservation efforts that make these parks so special.

As we explore together, I hope to ignite your passion for the national parks and encourage you to immerse yourself in the beauty of nature. Doing so can foster a greater awareness of the need to protect these precious landscapes for future generations. Let's embark on this adventure and discover nature's healing power and the mysteries that make these parks even more captivating.

## Your Adventure Begins Here

As you turn the pages of this book, I hope you'll feel the call of the wild and the urge to lace up your hiking boots, pack your camera, and embark on your journey through the Pacific's national parks. These parks are more than just destinations—they are places of wonder, reflection, and connection to nature's beauty. So, whether planning your next big adventure or simply exploring from the comfort of your favorite reading nook, this book is your gateway to some of the most awe-inspiring landscapes our planet offers.

Happy exploring, and may you find both inspiration and solace in the natural world.

ONE

# Yosemite National Park

## A CATHEDRAL OF GRANITE AND WATERFALLS

 *"The mountains are calling, and I must go."*

John Muir

Nestled in California's Sierra Nevada mountains, Yosemite National Park is a world-renowned sanctuary of towering granite cliffs, thundering waterfalls, and ancient sequoia groves. Its breathtaking landscapes have inspired generations of visitors, artists, and conservationists, drawing them into a realm where nature's grandeur is on full display. The park's story, however, begins long before it was designated as a national park in 1890.

For thousands of years, the Ahwahnechee (ah-wah-NEE-chee) people called this valley home, living harmoniously with the land and fostering a deep connection to the natural world. They hunted in the meadows, gathered acorns and other resources, and honored the sacred sites scattered throughout the landscape, which held cultural and spiritual significance.

The name "Yosemite" derives from the Miwok word for "those who kill," referring to the fierce tribes who once inhabited the area. Yet, the Ahwahnechee themselves referred to the valley as "Ahwahnee," meaning "gaping mouth," a term that reflects the awe and reverence they felt for the natural beauty surrounding them. Their understanding of the land was profound, as they practiced sustainable hunting and gathering methods that allowed them to thrive without depleting resources. The valley was not just a place to live; it was a sacred space filled with stories, legends, and a profound sense of belonging.

The park's transformation from an indigenous homeland to a national treasure began in the mid-19th century when European American settlers and gold seekers flooded California during the Gold Rush. This influx of newcomers brought significant changes to the landscape and disrupted the traditional ways of life for the Ahwahnechee. Early explorers, such as Lafayette Bunnell, documented the area's stunning landscapes, sparking interest among artists and photographers who began to capture the raw beauty of Yosemite's granite monoliths and cascading waterfalls. Bunnell's writings and vivid descriptions played a crucial role in introducing the natural wonders of Yosemite to a broader audience.

Among those captivated by Yosemite was John Muir, a name you'll encounter repeatedly throughout this book. Muir, a passionate naturalist, devoted his life to studying and advocating for preserving the park's unique ecosystems. His writings on Yosemite's majestic scenery galvanized public support for the preservation of wild lands, capturing readers' imaginations and influencing public policy. Muir's lyrical descriptions painted Yosemite as a paradise on earth, urging people to appreciate its beauty and recognize the urgent need for conservation.

In 1903, Muir's friendship with President Theodore Roosevelt led to a historic camping trip in Yosemite. This further solidified Roosevelt's commitment to conservation. The pair spent three days exploring the park, where Muir shared his profound knowledge of the landscape and its ecological importance. Inspired by Muir's passion and the awe-inspiring beauty of the park, Roosevelt became a strong advocate for the preservation of Yosemite and other national treasures. His efforts culminated in establishing Yosemite as a protected area, solidifying its place in the national consciousness as a symbol of unspoiled wilderness.

Yosemite's cultural significance extends beyond its scenic grandeur. The park has served as a spiritual haven for centuries, with sacred sites and traditional practices still honored by Native American tribes today. The towering granite walls of El Capitan and Half Dome are not just climbing challenges; they are revered landmarks imbued with cultural meaning, and stories passed down through generations. These rock formations hold significant spiritual value, symbolizing strength and resilience in adversity.

Efforts to conserve Yosemite's natural beauty continue today, with ongoing projects aimed at restoring meadows, protecting wildlife habitats, and mitigating the impact of millions of annual visitors. The park's diverse ecosystems, including ancient giant sequoias, lush meadows, and granite cliffs, support various plant and animal species. Conservationists are actively working to protect these habitats from invasive species, climate change, and tourism pressures. As one of the first areas in the United States to be set aside for preservation, Yosemite stands as a testament to the enduring power of nature and the importance of protecting our wild spaces.

The legacy of Yosemite is one of resilience and renewal, echoing the timeless connection between people and the land. Visitors traverse the park's trails, gaze at the cascading waterfalls, and stand in awe of the towering cliffs. They are not merely spectators but part of a vibrant blend of history, culture, and nature. Each step taken in Yosemite is an opportunity to connect with the land, reflect on its past, and honor the generations who came before us.

This book aims to be your guide in uncovering the many layers of Yosemite's story, revealing the magic of this national treasure and inspiring you to appreciate the beauty and significance of our natural world. As we delve deeper into the park's breathtaking landscapes and rich cultural heritage, may you be inspired to not only explore these wonders but also to foster a sense of stewardship for the environment we all share.

## Fascinating Facts About Yosemite

Yosemite National Park is a treasure trove of natural wonders and historical significance. Here are some intriguing facts that highlight the park's unique features and rich heritage:

1. **Established in 1890:** Yosemite was one of the first national parks in the United States, designated in 1890. It played a crucial role in the conservation movement, setting a precedent for protecting natural landscapes.
2. **Home to Giant Sequoias**: Yosemite is famous for its giant sequoias, including the Grizzly Giant, one of the oldest living trees in the world, estimated to be over 2,700 years old.
3. **Granite Monoliths**: The park's iconic granite formations, such as El Capitan and Half Dome, are popular among climbers. El Capitan rises over 3,000 feet (900 meters) straight up and is considered one of the ultimate challenges for rock climbers.

4. **Diverse Ecosystems**: Yosemite is home to several distinct ecosystems, ranging from lush meadows and forests to granite cliffs and alpine tundra. This biodiversity supports a wide variety of wildlife, including black bears, mule deer, and over 400 species of vertebrates.

5. **Waterfalls Galore**: Yosemite is home to some of the tallest waterfalls in North America. Yosemite Falls, which plunges 2,425 feet (739 meters), is the highest waterfall in the United States.

6. **Unique Geology**: The park's stunning landscape was shaped by glaciers during the last Ice Age, which carved out the valleys and created many of the park's features. Today's U-shaped valleys and granite cliffs directly result from this glacial activity.

7. **Cultural Significance**: The Ahwahnechee people, Native Americans who lived in the Yosemite Valley for thousands of years, have a rich cultural history. Their traditions and connection to the land remain integral to the park's identity.

8. **Dark Sky Parks**: Yosemite is designated a Dark Sky Park. It is recognized for its efforts to preserve the night sky and reduce light pollution, making it ideal for stargazing.

9. **Biodiversity Hotspot**: The park contains over 1,500 species of flowering plants, 400 species of vertebrates, and numerous species of fungi and bacteria. This diversity makes Yosemite a significant site for ecological research.

10. **Sustainable Practices**: Yosemite has implemented several sustainability initiatives, including reducing waste, conserving water, and protecting wildlife habitats, to ensure the park remains a pristine natural environment for future generations.

## Key Highlights and Must-See Landmarks

The heart of Yosemite beats most vividly in Yosemite Valley, a lush, seven-mile-long corridor surrounded by some of the world's most iconic rock formations. As you enter the valley, the first sight of El Capitan rising 3,000 feet above the Merced River is breathtaking. This colossal granite monolith is not just a rock but a sheer wall of ancient stone, streaked with water stains and bathed in the changing light of the day. Climbing enthusiasts from around the globe are drawn here, scaling its face in daring ascents that can take days to complete. Watching climbers move methodically up the rock, mere specks against the vastness of El Capitan, is an awe-inspiring sight, a testament to human perseverance against nature's raw, unyielding force.

Glacier Point, another of Yosemite's crown jewels, offers a panoramic view that stretches across the valley, showcasing Half Dome's unmistakable silhouette, a giant granite dome cleaved in half, seemingly sliced by a cosmic hand. Standing at Glacier Point, 3,200 feet above Curry Village, it feels as if you're at the edge of the world, with the valley floor far below and the High Sierra stretching endlessly into the horizon. At sunset, the entire scene is bathed in a golden glow, the sky ablaze with shades of pink and orange, and the granite peaks glowing as if lit from within.

No visit to Yosemite is complete without witnessing its majestic waterfalls. Yosemite Falls, the tallest waterfall in North America, plunges 2,425 feet from the top of the valley in a dramatic display of power and grace. When the snowmelt is at its peak in spring, the falls roar so intensely that mist fills the air, and rainbows dance in the spray. Nearby, Bridalveil Fall flows year-round, spilling gracefully over a sheer cliff, often casting a delicate veil of mist that gave it its name. The waterfall's base is easily accessible, and a short walk-through towering pines leads you to a viewpoint where you can feel the cool spray on your skin—a refreshing reminder of nature's raw energy.

Beyond the iconic sights, Yosemite is also rich in cultural history. The Ahwahnee Hotel, a grand lodge built in the 1920s, reflects the park's commitment to preserving its natural beauty while accommodating visitors in style. Designed to blend seamlessly with its surroundings, the hotel's stone walls, wooden beams, and expansive windows frame views of the surrounding cliffs, making it one of the most sought-after accommodations in the park. The hotel has hosted presidents, royalty, and celebrities, all drawn by the same timeless allure that captivated John Muir.

## Hidden Gems: Lesser-Known Spots Worth Exploring

While Yosemite's main attractions draw the crowds, hidden corners of the park offer solitude and a sense of discovery. One such spot is Taft Point, a lesser-known overlook that provides jaw-dropping views of El Capitan and the Yosemite Valley below. A short but rewarding hike through a forest of firs and pines leads to the cliff's edge, where the valley floor drops away. A network of fissures in the rock known as the "Fissures" opens beneath your feet. Unlike the busy viewpoints at Glacier Point, Taft Point often offers a quiet, contemplative space to take in the grandeur of the park without the bustle of the crowds.

The Mist Trail to Vernal and Nevada Falls is a must-do for those seeking a thrilling and immersive Yosemite experience. This 7-mile (11.3 km) round-trip hike gains about 2,000 feet (610 meters) in elevation, making it a moderately strenuous adventure that rewards hikers with stunning views at every turn. Starting at Happy Isles in Yosemite Valley, the trail immediately immerses you in the park's vibrant ecosystem as you wind alongside the

Merced River, whose waters roar and tumble over smooth granite boulders.

The first significant landmark is Vernal Fall, a 317-foot (97-meter) waterfall that thunders down with incredible force. The trail to Vernal Falls is steep and consists of over 600 stone steps carved directly into the rock, making for a challenging ascent that leaves you breathless in more ways than one. The constant spray from the falls can soak you to the skin, and on sunny days, the mist refracts the light into vibrant rainbows that arch across the trail—a truly magical sight. The air here is filled with the sound of crashing water and the scent of wet stone, creating a sensory experience that feels both refreshing and exhilarating.

The trail becomes more rugged and steep as you continue upward, but the beauty only intensifies. Upon reaching the top of Vernal Fall, you are greeted with a sweeping view down into the gorge, where the river flows gently before plunging over the edge. The trail then levels out briefly as you approach Nevada Fall, another spectacular sight. This 594-foot (181 meters) waterfall is even more dramatic, cascading down a sheer granite face and sending up a fine mist that nourishes the surrounding ferns and wildflowers.

The hike up to Nevada Falls includes more switchbacks and rocky terrain, with the trail clinging to the mountainside and offering dramatic vistas of the valley below. The air grows cooler and crisper as you gain elevation, and the towering granite walls surrounding the trail remind you of the immense forces that shaped this landscape. The final push to the top of Nevada Fall is a test of endurance, but the reward is worth every step. At the summit, you can rest and enjoy the panoramic views of Yosemite's rugged backcountry, where granite peaks rise against the blue sky, and the roar of the waterfalls echoes in the distance.

This trail is rated as difficult due to its steep climbs, rocky footing, and the physical demands of constant elevation gain. However, the effort is richly rewarded with some of the most iconic sights in Yosemite, making it a favorite among those who seek a hike that feels both challenging and deeply connected to the park's wild, untamed spirit.

Another hidden gem is the serene and often overlooked Mariposa Grove of Giant Sequoias. Located near the park's southern entrance, the grove is home to over 500 mature giant sequoias, some of which have stood for over 2,000 years. Walking among these ancient giants, with their massive trunks and towering canopies, is a humbling experience. The trees seem to whisper the secrets of centuries, their thick bark resistant to fire and time. The peacefulness of the grove, far from the busier areas of the park, provides a deep sense of connection to the natural world.

## Hiking Trails

Yosemite is a hiker's paradise, offering trails that range from gentle valley strolls to grueling climbs that test even the most seasoned adventurers. The first one we will talk about is Half Dome.

### Half Dome

Length: 14 to 16 miles (22.5 to 25.7 km) round-trip
Elevation Change: 4,800 feet (1,463 meters)
Difficulty: Strenuous

One of the most iconic hikes is the trek to the top of Half Dome, this legendary trek in Yosemite National Park is a journey that tests both body and mind, yet rewards with breathtaking views and an exhilarating sense of accomplishment. The 14- to 16-mile

(22.5 to 25.7 km) round-trip hike begins in the serene early morning hours, often shrouded in mist, as you step onto the Mist Trail. The first leg of the hike will take you alongside the roaring Merced River, with the trail cutting through lush forests of pine and oak, occasionally revealing glimpses of cascading waterfalls.

As you climb higher, you'll encounter Vernal Fall, a 317-foot (97-meter) water curtain that crashes into emerald pools below, often creating rainbows that dance in the sunlight. The trail here is steep and rocky, with countless granite steps that challenge your legs and test your stamina. You'll be enveloped in the cooling spray of the falls, a welcome respite from the exertion and a reminder of nature's raw power.

Continuing onward, you'll reach Nevada Fall, where the water thunders down 594 feet (181 meters), sending up a mist that nourishes the surrounding ferns and moss-covered rocks. The trail becomes a bit quieter here as the sound of the falls fades, and you find yourself surrounded by towering granite walls and rugged terrain. This is a place of contrasts, where the tranquility of nature meets the thrill of adventure.

The journey then transitions into Little Yosemite Valley, a relatively flat area where hikers often take a break to refuel. Here, you'll be greeted by sweeping views of the valley floor and the sight of Half Dome looming in the distance—your ultimate destination. The valley's expansive meadows and pine forests provide a serene backdrop. Still, there's no mistaking the challenge that lies ahead as the massive granite dome rises against the sky.

As you ascend toward the subdome, the terrain becomes more rugged, with switchbacks that zigzag through a landscape of jagged rocks and hardy shrubs. The air thins, making each step more deliberate. Upon reaching the Subdome, the trees thin out, and the granite expanse of Half Dome's face comes into full view, rising steeply and seemingly insurmountable.

The final stretch—the cables section—truly sets Half Dome apart. Here, you'll find two steel cables that are handrails anchored into the rock, guiding you up the nearly vertical ascent. The climb is nerve-wracking as you cling to the cables with all your strength, your feet searching for traction on the slick, smooth granite. The exposure is dizzying; a slip would mean a dangerous fall. Below, Yosemite's valleys stretch out like a vast, rugged tapestry, the trees reduced to specks.

Reaching the summit is a euphoric moment. Standing atop Half Dome, you are greeted by an unparalleled 360-degree panorama of Yosemite's granite wilderness—El Capitan to the west, Clouds Rest to the northeast, and the distant Sierra Nevada peaks on the horizon. The view is breathtaking, not just for its sheer beauty but for the sense of triumph it represents. Up here, 5,000 feet above the valley floor, you are truly on top of the world, surrounded by nature's grandeur and the quiet hum of the wind.

*Valley Loop Trail*

Length: 13 miles (20.9 km)
Elevation Change: Minimal
Difficulty: Moderate

For those looking for something less strenuous, the Valley Loop Trail offers a scenic 13-mile (20.9 km) loop around the valley floor, taking in sights like El Capitan, Bridalveil Fall, and the Merced River. With little elevation change, this trail provides a leisurely way to experience Yosemite's majesty up close, weaving through meadows filled with wildflowers in the spring and beneath the towering cliffs that have made the park famous.

*Four-Mile Trail*

Length: 4.8 miles (7.7 km) one-way
Elevation Change: 3,200 feet (975 meters)
Difficulty: Strenuous

The Four-Mile Trail, ironically closer to five miles in length, offers a steep ascent from the valley floor to Glacier Point, climbing nearly 3,200 feet (975 meters) in just over four miles (6.4 km). The switchbacks cut through forested slopes and rocky outcrops, revealing ever-expanding views of Yosemite Falls, Half Dome, and the distant High Sierra. Though challenging, the Four-Mile Trail provides one of the most rewarding hikes in the park, ending with the breathtaking panoramic views at Glacier Point.

## Other Activities: Beyond the Trails – Exploring Yosemite's Many Adventures

While hiking might be one of Yosemite's main attractions, the park offers many other activities catering to adventurers. From rock climbing on world-famous granite walls to leisurely floats down the Merced River, Yosemite is a playground for outdoor pursuits far beyond the trailhead.

### Rock Climbing: Scaling the Giants

For thrill-seekers and climbing enthusiasts, Yosemite is a mecca of vertical adventure. The park's massive granite cliffs, particularly El Capitan and Half Dome, draw climbers from around the world eager to test their skills on some of the most challenging routes on the planet. Whether you're an experienced climber tackling the towering face of El Capitan or a beginner trying your hand at a climbing lesson with one of Yosemite's local climbing schools, the sense of accomplishment from conquering these natural giants is unmatched. Yosemite Mountaineering School offers classes for all levels, allowing visitors to experience the exhilaration of climbing in one of the sport's most iconic destinations.

*Water Activities: Rafting, Swimming, and Fishing*

During the warmer months, the Merced River becomes a refreshing escape from the heat, winding lazily through Yosemite Valley and offering rafting, swimming, and even fishing opportunities. Rent a raft from the Yosemite Valley Lodge and float down the gentle current, taking in stunning views of El Capitan, Cathedral Rocks, and Yosemite Falls as you drift along. For a more tranquil experience, the park's numerous lakes and swimming holes, like Mirror Lake, provide idyllic spots to cool off and relax, surrounded by the towering granite walls that make Yosemite so iconic.

Fishing enthusiasts can try their luck at catching rainbow and brown trout in the park's rivers and streams. Fly fishing is particularly popular in areas like the Tuolumne River, where clear waters and stunning mountain backdrops create an unforgettable angling experience. Remember to check regulations and obtain a California fishing license before casting your line.

*Photography: Capturing the Majesty of Yosemite*

Yosemite's breathtaking landscapes have inspired countless photographers, from early pioneers like Ansel Adams to modern-day visitors looking to capture the perfect shot. Whether you're a professional photographer or just capturing memories with your smartphone, the park offers endless opportunities to snap stunning photos. Sunrise and sunset are particularly magical times when the light bathes the granite cliffs in warm, golden hues, and the park's waterfalls glow with soft pastels. Popular photography spots include Tunnel View, where you can capture the entire valley with El Capitan, Bridalveil Fall, and Half Dome all in one frame, and Glacier Point, where sweeping vistas stretch as far as the eye can see.

For those looking to refine their skills, the Ansel Adams Gallery offers photography classes and workshops where you can learn tips and techniques to make the most of your time behind the lens. There's no shortage of subjects in Yosemite—from the grandiose to the delicate details of wildflowers and wildlife, every corner of the park holds a picture waiting to be taken.

### *Stargazing: A Celestial Spectacle*

When the sun sets behind the granite peaks, Yosemite transforms into one of the best stargazing spots in California. With minimal light pollution, the night sky reveals a stunning array of stars, planets, and even the Milky Way, visible to the naked eye on clear nights. Head to Glacier Point for a front-row seat to the cosmos, where the vastness of the sky stretches above you, unobstructed by city lights. During the summer, park rangers and astronomers often host stargazing programs, complete with telescopes and guided night sky tours.

### *Winter Activities: Snowshoeing, Skiing, and Ice Skating*

Yosemite's winter wonderland is a paradise for those who enjoy cold-weather activities. When the snow blankets the park, Badger Pass Ski Area becomes a hub for downhill skiing and snowboarding, offering a more relaxed and family-friendly alternative to larger ski resorts. For a quieter experience, try snowshoeing or cross-country skiing through the park's serene, snow-draped meadows and forests.

One of the most picturesque winter activities is ice skating at the Curry Village Ice Rink. The stunning backdrop of Half Dome creates a magical setting. Surrounded by snow-capped peaks, skating under the open sky is a truly memorable way to experience Yosemite in the winter.

*Wildlife Watching: A Glimpse of Yosemite's Inhabitants*

Wildlife watching is a year-round activity in Yosemite, and the park's diverse habitats are home to a wide array of animals. Early mornings and late afternoons are the best times to spot mule deer grazing in meadows, black bears foraging in the forest, or coyotes trotting along the valley floor. Binoculars are a must for bird-watchers, as the park hosts over 250 species of birds, including the vibrant Steller's jay, the majestic bald eagle, and the agile peregrine falcon. Spotting these creatures in their natural habitat is a reminder of the wildness that still thrives in this protected landscape.

*Ranger-Led Programs: Discover Yosemite's Secrets*

Yosemite's ranger-led programs are a great way to deepen your connection to the park. From nature walks that explore the park's unique geology and ecosystems to evening campfire talks that dive into the park's history and wildlife, these programs provide a wealth of knowledge and insight. The Junior Ranger Program is perfect for young adventurers, offering a chance for kids to learn about the park's natural wonders while earning a Junior Ranger badge.

These activities are just a taste of what Yosemite offers beyond its legendary hiking trails. Whether scaling a granite wall, floating down a river, or simply soaking in the scenery, Yosemite invites you to explore its many facets and adventure in its vast, awe-inspiring landscape.

## Flora and Fauna: The Park's Diverse Ecosystems

Yosemite's varied landscapes host incredible plant and animal life diversity, with ecosystems ranging from oak woodlands to alpine tundra. The park's flora is highlighted by the iconic giant sequoias, some of the earth's largest and oldest trees. These ancient giants dominate the Mariposa, Tuolumne, and Merced groves, towering over all other vegetation. In spring, Yosemite Valley bursts into color as wildflowers blanket the meadows—lupines, Indian paintbrush, and California poppies create a vibrant tapestry against the backdrop of granite walls.

Yosemite is also home to an array of wildlife, from the elusive black bears that roam the forests to the mule deer grazing in the meadows. Birdwatchers can spot peregrine falcons soaring above the cliffs or the striking Steller's jay with its vivid blue plumage flitting among the pines. The park's diverse habitats support over 400 species of animals, including rare sightings of bobcats, mountain lions, and even the occasional Sierra Nevada red fox, one of the rarest carnivores in North America.

## Best Campgrounds and Accommodation Options

For those wishing to extend their Yosemite adventure, the park offers a variety of camping and accommodation options. Camp 4, the historic campground at the base of El Capitan, is a must for rock climbers and those seeking to immerse themselves in the climbing culture that has defined Yosemite for decades. For a more serene experience, Upper Pines Campground offers sites nestled among pine trees, with easy access to the valley's main attractions.

The Ahwahnee Hotel, Yosemite's premier lodge, provides a touch of luxury amidst the wilderness, with stunning views, fine dining, and historic charm. For those seeking backcountry solitude, Yosemite's wilderness permits allow access to remote campsites far from the crowds, where the stars shine bright, and the only sound is the rustle of the wind through the trees.

## Mystical Encounters: Legends of Yosemite

Yosemite National Park is steeped in enchanting tales and mystical experiences that continue to captivate visitors. One such story involves the ghost of Mary Curry, a park resident in the early 1900s. Mary arrived in Yosemite seeking a fresh start and quickly became a beloved figure among the local community. Known for her warm smile and generosity, she worked tirelessly to establish one of the first lodges in Curry Village, welcoming visitors nationwide.

Tragically, Mary's life took a sorrowful turn. One autumn evening, she ventured out to gather wildflowers but lost her way as a sudden storm swept through the area. Disoriented by the swirling mist and darkness, she tragically perished in the wilderness, leaving the community heartbroken.

Mary's spirit is said to linger in the park, with visitors reporting encounters with her ghostly figure, often described as shimmering in white. Many who have seen her felt a sense of calm and warmth as if she were still offering her hospitality. One memorable encounter occurred in the summer of 2015 when a couple camping near Curry Village noticed a soft glow from the lodge. They approached and saw a woman in white, illuminated by the moonlight, only to have her vanish when they got closer.

Another visitor, a park ranger named Jake, shared his experience during a night patrol. "I felt a sudden chill despite the warm night," he recounted. "Walking past the lodge, I saw a faint light flickering inside. When I entered, the room was empty. It felt like I had just missed something magical."

These encounters with Mary Curry remind visitors of the deep history and enduring legends woven into Yosemite's fabric.

### The Enchanted Lake

Another mystical tale tells of a hidden lake in Yosemite's wilderness, the Enchanted Lake. According to local lore, this lake appears only under specific conditions—typically during a full moon or after heavy rains. Visitors who have stumbled upon it describe the water as shimmering with an ethereal light, inducing a sense of tranquility and connection to nature. Some claim that rare creatures can be seen around the lake, hinting at its status as a portal to another realm. Those fortunate enough to find the lake often describe it as a transformative experience that leaves them with a profound sense of peace and wonder.

## *Bigfoot Sightings*

Yosemite has also become a hotspot for sightings of Bigfoot, the legendary creature said to roam the forests of North America. Over the years, numerous visitors have reported encounters, often describing large footprints, strange sounds echoing through the trees, or glimpses of a massive figure disappearing into the underbrush. While skeptics may question these claims, the stories persist, adding an air of mystery to the park's allure. One visitor reported hearing eerie calls in the distance while camping in a secluded area, sparking conversations around the campfire about what might be lurking just beyond the trees.

These stories, blending fact and folklore, invite visitors to explore Yosemite's stunning landscapes and the mystical qualities that make this national treasure a place of wonder.

## Practical Travel Tips and Planning Information

Yosemite is a year-round destination, offering its unique experience each season. Spring brings roaring waterfalls, while summer is ideal for hiking and camping. Fall provides a quieter, less crowded experience with beautiful autumn foliage, and winter transforms the park into a snowy wonderland perfect for skiing and snowshoeing. Be sure to pack layers, as temperatures vary greatly between day and night, and always carry plenty of water, especially in the warmer months.

Navigating Yosemite can be challenging, especially during peak season. Arrive early to find parking and consider using the park's shuttle service to avoid traffic congestion. Safety is paramount— stay on marked trails, keep a safe distance from wildlife, and always be bear-aware. Planning will ensure you make the most of your time in this extraordinary place, whether you're here for a day or a week.

## Conclusion: Inspiring Further Exploration

Yosemite is more than just a park; it's a living masterpiece of nature's finest work. As you explore its towering cliffs, meandering rivers, and quiet groves, take a moment to reflect on the history, the beauty, and the efforts that have preserved this place for generations. Let Yosemite's landscapes inspire you to seek out your own adventures, tread lightly, and continue the conservation legacy that keeps these wonders alive. So go ahead, explore, and find your own connection to this breathtaking cathedral of granite and waterfalls.

# TWO

# Sequoia National Park

## LAND OF GIANTS AND TIMELESS BEAUTY

*"The conservation of natural resources is the fundamental problem. Unless we solve that problem, it will avail us little to solve all others."*

President Theodore Roosevelt

## Introduction

Sequoia National Park, nestled in California's southern Sierra Nevada mountains, is a realm where time seems to stretch and ancient giants tower over the landscape. Established in 1890, this park is home to some of the largest trees on Earth, including the famous General Sherman Tree. This colossal Sequoia has stood for over two millennia. However, the history of Sequoia extends far beyond its designation as a national park; it is a land rich with stories of indigenous cultures, early explorers, and a conservation movement that fought to protect these natural wonders from the relentless push of industrialization.

Long before settlers set their sights on the towering sequoias, the land was inhabited by Native American tribes, including the Monache (moh-NAH-chee) and Yokuts (YOH-kuts) peoples. These tribes lived in the shadow of the giant trees, utilizing the land's resources for food, medicine, and shelter. The sequoias were not merely trees but sacred beings, standing as silent witnesses to centuries of tradition and life. Native Americans used the area's abundant plants for food and medicinal purposes. They hunted in the rich forests, leaving behind grinding stones and pictographs that still whisper tales of their presence.

In the mid-19th century, the lure of California's gold brought an influx of settlers and explorers into the Sierra Nevada. Among them was Hale Tharp, a cattle rancher who became the first European American to enter what is now Sequoia National Park. Tharp stumbled upon a meadow surrounded by the towering giants and was so taken by its beauty that he established a summer retreat, living in a hollowed-out sequoia log that still stands today, known as Tharp's Log. As settlers began to encroach on the land, the threat of logging loomed over the ancient trees. The park's sequoias, with their massive trunks and incredible height, were seen as prime targets for timber.

The battle to protect Sequoia's ancient giants from logging was not easily won. Early conservationists, inspired by the writings of John Muir and alarmed by the rapid deforestation occurring throughout California, lobbied fiercely for the park's protection. In 1890, their efforts paid off when Sequoia National Park was established, making it the second national park in the United States, created just days before its neighbor, Yosemite. The park's establishment marked a significant victory for the nascent conservation movement, setting a precedent for preserving natural wonders nationwide. This achievement is a testament to the power of collective action and the enduring legacy of those who fought for the park's protection.

Sequoia National Park's cultural significance is deeply intertwined with its natural splendor. The park is home to sacred sites and historical landmarks, including the ancient sequoia groves with centuries of history within their thick, fire-resistant bark. The Kaweah (kuh-WEE-uh) Colony, a utopian socialist community, attempted to settle in the area in the late 19th century, attracted by the grandeur of the trees. Though their endeavor ultimately failed, the colony's legacy can still be seen in place names and old trails, a reminder of the many lives that have been touched by this land.

Conservation efforts continue to play a crucial role in Sequoia's story. The park's ecosystems face modern challenges, including climate change, drought, and wildfire. To combat these threats, ongoing restoration projects focus on preserving the delicate balance of the forest, protecting wildlife habitats, and reducing the impact of invasive species. Efforts to restore fire to the landscape through controlled burns help maintain the health of the sequoia groves, mimicking the natural fire cycles that the trees depend on for regeneration. As a testament to these efforts, Sequoia National Park stands today as a symbol of resilience. In this place, ancient giants continue to thrive against the odds.

## Fascinating Facts About Sequoia National Park

1. **Home to the Largest Trees**: Sequoia National Park is famous for its giant sequoias, the largest trees on Earth by volume. The General Sherman Tree, located in the park, is the largest living tree in the world.

1. **Ancient Giants:** Some of the sequoias in the park are over 3,000 years old, meaning they were already ancient during the time of the Roman Empire.
2. **Established in 1890**: Sequoia National Park was established in 1890, making it the second national park in the United States, following Yellowstone.
3. **Unique Ecosystems**: The park encompasses a variety of ecosystems, including lush meadows, alpine regions, and rugged mountains, supporting diverse wildlife and plant species.
4. **High Elevation**: Mount Whitney, the highest peak in the contiguous United States at 14,505 feet (4,421 meters), is located just outside the park's boundaries. The park ranges from 1,300 to 14,494 feet (396 to 4,421 meters).
5. **Glacial Carving**: Glaciers during the last Ice Age shaped the stunning landscapes of Sequoia, creating deep canyons and dramatic granite cliffs.
6. **Fire-Resistant Trees**: Sequoias have thick, fire-resistant bark that can be up to 3 feet (0.9 meters) thick, allowing them to survive many wildfires that occur in their habitat.
7. **Rare Flora:** In addition to the giant sequoias, the park features several unique plant species, including the Sequoia sempervirens (coastal redwood), which is found only in California.
8. **Largest Living Organism**: The General Sherman Tree is not just the largest tree by volume; it is also considered one of the largest living organisms on Earth, with a trunk volume of over 52,500 cubic feet (1,487 cubic meters).
9. **Caving Adventures**: The park is home to several caves, including the famous Crystal Cave, which features stunning formations and offers guided tours for visitors.

## Key Highlights and Must-See Landmarks

Sequoia National Park is a place of awe and wonder, where the scale of the natural world can make even the tallest visitor feel small. The General Sherman Tree stands out as a true marvel among its many highlights. At 275 feet tall and over 36 feet in diameter at the base (no that is not a typo), General Sherman is not the tallest or the widest tree in the world. Still, it is the largest by volume, containing more wood than any other living tree. Standing before it, you are dwarfed by its massive trunk, the reddish bark glowing warmly in the dappled sunlight. There's a sense of timelessness here as if this ancient tree has seen centuries unfold beneath its boughs.

Nearby, the Giant Forest has more than 8,000 colossal sequoias, creating an otherworldly landscape of towering trunks and expansive canopies. As you wander through the grove, the air is filled with the rich scent of pine and earth, and the sound of the wind rustling through the leaves creates a symphony of nature. The towering trees stretch towards the sky, their massive branches casting cool shadows on the forest floor below. The peacefulness of the grove is palpable, offering a serene escape from the busier areas of the park.

Moro Rock, a massive granite dome rising 6,725 feet above sea level, offers one of the most breathtaking panoramic views in the park. A steep staircase carved into the rock leads to the summit, where a sweeping vista of the Great Western Divide, the Kaweah River, and the surrounding valleys unfolds. The climb is exhilarating, with each step revealing more of the stunning landscape. At the top, the wind whips around you, and the vast expanse of the Sierra Nevada stretches out in every direction—a perfect reward for the climb.

Tunnel Log is another must-see. It is a fallen sequoia hollowed out in 1937 to allow cars to pass through. Driving under the enormous trunk is a fun and quirky experience that captures the sheer scale of the park's trees. For a more tranquil encounter, visit Crescent Meadow, described by John Muir as the "Gem of the Sierra." This lush, flower-filled meadow, encircled by sequoias, provides a peaceful setting where deer graze and wildflowers bloom in vibrant bursts of color.

## Hidden Gems: Lesser-Known Spots Worth Exploring

While the main attractions draw the crowds, Sequoia National Park is also home to quieter, lesser-known spots that offer solitude and unique experiences. One such hidden gem is the serene Muir Grove, a secluded collection of giant sequoias accessible via a moderate, 4-mile (6.4 km) round-trip hike through pine forests and rocky outcrops. Unlike the busier groves, Muir Grove is often empty, allowing visitors to wander among the trees in peaceful solitude, listening to the soft crunch of pine needles underfoot and the occasional call of a woodpecker tapping at a tree trunk.

Marble Falls, a cascading waterfall tucked away in the park's foothills, offers a stunning reward for those willing to venture off the beaten path. The 8-mile (12.9 km) round-trip hike to the falls winds through chaparral and oak woodlands, with bursts of wild-flowers in the spring. The trail is less frequented than others, allowing one to experience the park's beauty away from the crowds. The falls are a striking sight, with water tumbling over smooth, marble-like rock, creating a series of small pools perfect for a refreshing dip on a warm day.

For those interested in the park's history, the old Colony Mill Road, once used by the Kaweah Colony, offers a glimpse into the past. The trail follows the route of a historic wagon road, winding through forests and offering views of the Kaweah River. Along the way, interpretive signs tell the story of the colony's ambitious but ultimately doomed attempt to establish a utopian community in the shadow of the sequoias.

## Hiking Trails

Sequoia National Park offers diverse hiking trails, from gentle strolls among the giants to challenging ascents with panoramic views. Each trail provides a unique opportunity to immerse yourself in the park's stunning landscapes and towering trees.

### *The Congress Trail*

Length: 2 miles (3.2 km) round-trip
Elevation Change: Minimal
Difficulty: Easy

The Congress Trail is a perfect introduction to the wonders of the Giant Forest. This easy, paved loop winds through some of the park's largest and most impressive trees, including the President, Chief Sequoyah, and McKinley trees. The trail meanders through the heart of the sequoia grove, where the sheer size of the trees is overwhelming. Walking beneath the massive branches, you can't help but feel a sense of reverence for these ancient beings that have stood for thousands of years. Interpretive signs along the way provide fascinating insights into the ecology of the sequoias and the conservation efforts that protect them.

### Tokopah Falls Trail

Length: 4 miles (6.4 km) round-trip
Elevation Change: 500 feet (152 meters)
Difficulty: Moderate

For a scenic hike that combines lush meadows, cascading rivers, and a stunning waterfall, the Tokopah Falls Trail is a must-do. The trail follows the Marble Fork of the Kaweah River, winding through forests and along rocky outcrops. The sound of rushing water accompanies you throughout the hike. The trail is alive in spring and early summer with wildflowers and butterflies. The final destination, Tokopah Falls, is a 1,200-foot (366-meter) cascade that tumbles dramatically down a granite cliff. Standing at the base of the falls, you can feel the cool mist on your face as the water crashes down—a refreshing reward for the journey.

### Lakes Trail to Pear Lake

Length: 12 miles (19.3 km) round-trip
Elevation Change: 2,200 feet (670 meters)
Difficulty: Strenuous

For experienced hikers looking for a more challenging adventure, the Lakes Trail to Pear Lake offers a full day's journey through some of the most beautiful high-altitude landscapes in the park. The trail begins at Wolverton and climbs steadily through alpine forests and meadows, passing by a series of shimmering mountain lakes, including Heather, Emerald, and Aster Lakes. The final destination, Pear Lake, is a serene alpine lake nestled in a granite basin surrounded by jagged peaks. The crystal-clear water reflects the surrounding landscape, creating a picture-perfect setting. Be prepared for changing weather conditions and pack plenty of water, as the high elevation can be demanding.

## Moro Rock Trail

Length: 0.5 miles (0.8 km) round-trip
Elevation Change: 300 feet (91 meters)
Difficulty: Moderate

One of the most iconic hikes in Sequoia, the Moro Rock Trail offers a short but exhilarating climb to the top of a granite dome with breathtaking views of the Sierra Nevada. The trail consists of a steep staircase carved into the rock, with railings to assist on the narrow sections. As you ascend, the views become more expansive, revealing the Kaweah River, deep canyons, and the Great Western Divide. Reaching the summit feels like standing on the edge of the world, with nothing but sky and mountains stretching out before you. It's a perfect hike for sunrise or sunset when the light casts a golden glow over the landscape.

## Alta Peak Trail

Length: 14 miles (22.5 km) round-trip
Elevation Change: 4,000 feet (1,219 meters)
Difficulty: Strenuous

The Alta Peak Trail is a challenging hike that rewards with one of the most spectacular views in Sequoia National Park. The trail begins at Wolverton and climbs steadily through dense pine and fir forests, emerging onto open ridges with panoramic vistas. The higher you climb, the more the landscape opens, revealing sweeping views of the Great Western Divide and the jagged peaks of the Sierra Nevada. The final ascent to Alta Peak is steep and exposed, but the 360-degree view from the summit is unparalleled. On a clear day, you can see all the way to Mount Whitney, the highest peak in the contiguous United States. This hike is best attempted by experienced hikers prepared for a long, strenuous day.

## Other Activities: Beyond the Trails – Experiencing Sequoia's Wonders

While hiking through Sequoia National Park is an unforgettable experience, numerous other activities allow visitors to fully immerse themselves in the park's breathtaking landscapes and rich history. Here are some exciting alternatives to explore during your visit:

### *Caving and Spelunking*

Sequoia National Park is home to several fascinating caves, most notably Crystal Cave, a stunning marble cavern featuring intricate rock formations and shimmering pools. Guided tours take you through the cave's winding passages, where you can marvel at stalactites, stalagmites, and unique mineral deposits. Tours typically last about 45 minutes and offer a cool retreat from the summer heat. Reserve your tickets in advance, as tours can fill up quickly during peak season.

### *Wildlife Watching*

The park's diverse ecosystems provide a wide range of wildlife habitat. From the towering giant sequoias to the alpine meadows, Sequoia is home to black bears, mule deer, bobcats, and various bird species, including the majestic golden eagle. Early morning or late afternoon are the best times for spotting wildlife. Consider taking a guided wildlife tour to learn more about the park's inhabitants and their behaviors, ensuring you have a safe and respectful experience while observing them in their natural habitat.

## Ranger-Led Programs

Participating in ranger-led programs is an excellent way to gain deeper insights into the park's history, ecology, and cultural significance. Rangers offers a variety of programs, including guided nature walks, campfire talks, and educational presentations that cover topics ranging from the giant sequoias' life cycle to the history of the Native American tribes that once inhabited the area. These programs provide an excellent opportunity to ask questions and engage with knowledgeable park staff.

## Photography

Sequoia National Park is a photographer's paradise, offering countless opportunities to capture stunning landscapes and unique wildlife. The golden light of sunrise and sunset transforms the giant sequoias, casting long shadows and illuminating the forest in warm hues. Popular photography spots include the Giant Forest, Moro Rock, and the meadows along Crescent Meadow Road. Don't forget your camera to document the breathtaking vistas and moments you'll encounter.

## Stargazing

With its high elevation and minimal light pollution, Sequoia National Park is an ideal location for stargazing. The park offers some of the clearest night skies in California, allowing you to witness the brilliance of the Milky Way and countless constellations. Popular stargazing spots include the summit of Moro Rock and the meadows near the Giant Forest. Join a ranger-led stargazing program to learn about celestial navigation and the mythology behind the stars.

### Horseback Riding

Exploring Sequoia on horseback offers a unique way to experience the park's beauty and tranquility. Several stables and outfitters provide guided horseback rides through scenic trails, allowing you to take in the stunning views of the giant sequoias and surrounding landscapes from a different perspective. Riding through the forest creates a sense of connection with nature. It offers a peaceful escape from the more crowded areas of the park.

### Fishing

Fishing in the park's pristine rivers and lakes can be a relaxing and rewarding experience. The lakes and streams in Sequoia are home to native species such as rainbow trout and brook trout. Popular fishing spots include the Kern River and several lakes scattered throughout the park. Be sure to check fishing regulations and obtain any necessary permits before you start and remember to practice catch-and-release to help preserve the park's aquatic ecosystems.

### Picnicking

Sequoia National Park features numerous picturesque picnic areas, allowing you to enjoy a meal surrounded by the beauty of nature. Popular spots include the Giant Forest and the area near Crescent Meadow. Bring a packed lunch and take a break from your adventures to soak in the serene atmosphere while listening to the sounds of the forest. Be sure to follow park regulations regarding waste disposal to keep the environment pristine.

Sequoia transforms into a snowy wonderland perfect for snow-shoeing and cross-country skiing in winter. The quiet, snow-covered forests provide a peaceful escape, with opportunities to spot winter wildlife such as deer, foxes, and even the occasional bear preparing for hibernation. The Wolverton Snowplay Area is ideal for families, offering a designated space for sledding and winter fun.

## Flora and Fauna: The Park's Diverse Ecosystems

Sequoia National Park is a biodiversity hotspot, home to various ecosystems ranging from lowland chaparral to high-altitude alpine zones. The park's most iconic residents are the giant sequoias, the largest trees on Earth by volume. These ancient giants thrive in the park's mid-elevation zones, where rich soil, ample moisture, and frequent fires create the perfect environment for their growth. The sequoias' thick, fibrous bark protects them from fire and insects, allowing them to live for thousands of years.

Beyond the sequoias, the park is rich with diverse plant life. In spring, meadows burst into bloom with vibrant wildflowers, including lupines, columbines, and California poppies. The park's higher elevations are characterized by hardy alpine plants, such as mountain heather and Sierra primrose, adapted to survive in the thin air and harsh conditions of the Sierra Nevada.

Wildlife abounds in Sequoia, with black bears, mule deer, and mountain lions among the larger mammals that roam the park. Smaller creatures, like marmots, squirrels, and various bird species, can be spotted throughout the year. The park's rivers and lakes are home to native trout, and keen-eyed visitors may spot peregrine falcons soaring above the granite cliffs. Sequoia's diverse ecosystems support an impressive array of life, each species playing a vital role in the park's complex web of nature.

## Best Campgrounds and Accommodation Options

Sequoia National Park offers several excellent camping options, from developed campgrounds with amenities to more primitive backcountry sites. Lodgepole Campground is one of the most popular, located along the Marble Fork of the Kaweah River. With easy access to the Giant Forest and nearby hiking trails, Lodgepole offers a convenient and scenic spot to set up camp. Sites are well-spaced among pines and offer amenities such as restrooms, picnic tables, and fire rings.

For those seeking a more rustic experience, Buckeye Flat Campground, set beside the Middle Fork of the Kaweah River, provides a quieter alternative with a more intimate connection to nature. Backcountry camping is also available for those exploring Sequoia's more remote areas. Permits are required, and hikers should be prepared for rugged conditions and practice Leave No Trace principles.

For those preferring a roof over their heads, the Wuksachi (wok-SAH-chee) Lodge offers comfortable accommodations with stunning views of the surrounding forest. The lodge's stone-and-cedar architecture blends beautifully with its natural surroundings, providing a cozy base to explore the park.

## Mystical Encounters: Legends of Sequoia

Sequoia National Park is known for its breathtaking landscapes and towering giant sequoias. Still, it is also steeped in tales of mystical encounters and unusual sightings that continue to captivate visitors.

### *The Whispering Pines: A Visitor's Account*

In the summer of 2015, a group of friends camped in a secluded area of Sequoia National Park. They set up their tents surrounded by towering giant sequoias. They spent the evening around a campfire, enjoying the natural beauty and sounds of the park.

As night fell, the group began to hear faint whispers carried by the wind. Initially, the sounds were soft and indistinct, but they grew clearer as the friends listened intently. One camper, Mike, noted, "It sounded like voices, almost melodic, drifting through the trees."

Intrigued by the phenomenon, the group decided to investigate the source of the whispers. They approached the nearby sequoias, where the sounds seemed to be emanating. However, as they moved closer, the whispers faded, leaving them with only the rustling leaves and the forest sounds.

Despite not finding a source for the voices, the campers felt a profound connection to the wilderness. Sarah, one of the friends, reflected, "It felt like the forest was trying to communicate with us, sharing its secrets."

The experience left a lasting impression on the group. They left Sequoia with a sense of wonder and a deeper appreciation for the mysteries of nature, highlighting the unique and sometimes mystical experiences that can occur in the park.

### *Mysterious Lights*

In 2018, a couple hiking in the Giant Forest reported seeing mysterious lights among the trees. "At first, we thought it was just our flashlights reflecting off something," the woman explained, "but the lights seemed to move on their own, dancing between the trees." The couple described the lights as orbs, glowing softly in the twilight. "It felt magical, like something out of a storybook," she said. While they could not explain what they saw, they were left with a sense of wonder.

### The Shadowy Figure

Another intriguing account comes from friends who went back-packing through Sequoia National Park in 2019. While setting up camp near the base of Mount Whitney, they reported seeing a shadowy figure lurking at the edge of the trees. "At first, we thought it was just another hiker, but when we called out, it didn't respond," one of the friends recalled. It just stood there, watching us."

The figure seemed to dissolve into the shadows when the group approached, leaving them bewildered. "We later discussed it, and some of us felt a chill as if we were being observed by something otherworldly," another friend added. The experience left them unsettled and fascinated, and they spent the rest of the night sharing ghost stories around the campfire.

## Practical Travel Tips and Planning Information

The best time to visit Sequoia is late spring through early fall when the weather is mild, and the park's trails are fully accessible. In winter, many areas, including Moro Rock, may be closed due to snow. Still, the park's snowy landscape offers a unique beauty. Packing layers is essential, as temperatures can vary greatly between day and night. Don't forget sturdy hiking boots, plenty of water, and sun protection.

Navigating Sequoia can be challenging, especially during peak season when parking is limited. Arrive early to secure a spot and consider using the free shuttle service that operates during the summer months. Remember to carry bear spray, store food properly, and always keep a safe distance from wildlife.

## Conclusion

Sequoia National Park is a testament to nature's grandeur and resilience. In this place, the giants of the forest stand tall against the passage of time. As you explore its towering sequoias, serene meadows, and rugged peaks, take a moment to reflect on the ancient history and conservation efforts that have protected this magnificent landscape. The park is not just a destination but a living, breathing monument to the enduring power of nature and the importance of preserving it for future generations.

Whether wandering through the quiet corners of Muir Grove, standing in awe beneath the General Sherman Tree, or feeling the cool spray of Tokopah Falls, Sequoia invites you to slow down and connect with the natural world. Let the park's timeless beauty inspire you to explore deeper, tread lightly, and appreciate the wild places that still exist in our modern world.

As you leave Sequoia, consider how you can contribute to its ongoing preservation—whether through volunteering, supporting park foundations, or simply practicing good stewardship during your visit. These actions, small as they may seem, help ensure that the giants of Sequoia will continue to stand for centuries to come, inspiring future generations to protect the natural wonders of our world. So go forth, explore, and let the majesty of Sequoia National Park fill your soul with a sense of wonder and a renewed commitment to the wild.

# THREE

# Joshua Tree National Park

## WHERE DESERT DREAMS MEET SKY

*"The beauty of the desert is a unique and inspiring experience."*

Bruce Springsteen, musician

### Introduction: The Park's History and Significance

Joshua Tree National Park, where two starkly different desert ecosystems converge, offers a landscape that feels other-worldly and familiar. Located in southeastern California, this vast expanse of rugged rock formations, spiky Joshua trees, and open desert plains has captured the imaginations of artists, adventurers, and spiritual seekers for centuries. The park's history is a rich mosaic shaped by the lives of Native American tribes, early explorers, miners, and conservationists who fought to preserve its unique beauty.

Long before the park was established, the area was home to Native American tribes such as the Serrano, Cahuilla (kah-WEE-yah), and

Chemehuevi (cheh-meh-WAY-vee), who adapted to the harsh desert environment with remarkable ingenuity. They utilized the land's resources for food, medicine, and shelter, leaving behind evidence of their presence in petroglyphs, rock art, and ancient trails that still wind through the desert today. The Joshua trees themselves, with their gnarled branches and spiky leaves, held significance for the indigenous peoples, who used the tree's fibrous leaves for baskets and sandals and its seeds and blossoms as a food source.

In the late 19th and early 20th centuries, prospectors and miners flocked to the region for gold, silver, and other valuable minerals. Remnants of this era can still be found scattered throughout the park—rusting mine shafts, stone cabins, and the weathered remains of old mining equipment stand as silent witnesses to the boom-and-bust cycles that once dominated the area. One of the most notable historical sites is the Lost Horse Mine, which produced over 10,000 ounces of gold and silver before it was abandoned in the early 1900s.

Despite its stark beauty, the desert landscape was not immediately recognized for its ecological and aesthetic value. In the 1930s, when a Pasadena socialite named Minerva Hoyt began advocating for the preservation of desert environments, the Joshua Tree region gained attention. Captivated by the unique flora and rugged landscapes, Hoyt launched a campaign to protect the area from the development and overharvesting of native plants. Her efforts were instrumental in creating the Joshua Tree National Monument in 1936, an initial step that protected over 800,000 acres of desert wilderness.

In 1994, the California Desert Protection Act elevated the monument to national park status. It expanded its boundaries and solidified its place as a cherished natural wonder. Today, Joshua Tree

National Park stands as a testament to the resilience of the desert and the enduring efforts of conservationists who recognized the need to protect this fragile landscape. The park's ecosystems face ongoing challenges, including climate change, drought, and the impact of increasing visitation. Conservation efforts focus on preserving the unique desert flora, restoring damaged habitats, and educating visitors about the importance of protecting this remarkable place.

Joshua Tree's cultural significance extends beyond its natural beauty. The park has long inspired artists, musicians, and spiritual seekers drawn to its stark, open spaces and haunting silence. From the rock formations of Skull Rock to the endless expanse of Cholla Cactus Garden, Joshua Tree is a place where nature and imagination collide, creating a landscape that feels ancient and timeless.

## Fascinating Facts About Joshua Tree National Park

1. **Established in 1994**: Joshua Tree National Park was designated as a national park on October 31, 1994, protecting over 790,000 acres of unique desert landscapes.
2. **Two Distinct Ecosystems**: The park features two main ecosystems: the Mojave Desert and the Colorado Desert. This diversity creates a wide range of flora and fauna.
3. **The Joshua Tree**: The park is named after the Joshua tree (Yucca brevifolia), which is not actually a tree but a species of yucca. These unique plants can live for over 150 years.
4. **Rock Climbing Haven**: Joshua Tree is known as a premier rock climbing destination. With over 8,000 climbing routes and bouldering opportunities, it attracts climbers from around the world.

1. **High Elevation**: The park's elevation ranges from about 1,000 feet (300 meters) to over 5,800 feet (1,800 meters) at Keys View, providing diverse habitats and stunning vistas.
2. **Temperature Extremes**: The park experiences significant temperature variations, with summer highs often exceeding 100°F (38°C) and winter lows dropping below freezing.
3. **Historic Gold Mining**: In the late 19th century, the area was a center for gold mining. The remnants of old mining camps can still be found within the park.
4. **Wildlife Crossings**: The park has several wildlife corridors, allowing animals to move safely between habitats, which is crucial for survival.
5. **Unique Geology**: The park features fascinating geological formations, including large boulders, rock piles, and the iconic Wonderland of Rocks, formed over millions of years by erosion.
6. **Stargazing Paradise**: Joshua Tree is designated as an International Dark Sky Park, making it an excellent location for stargazing due to its minimal light pollution.

## Key Highlights and Must-See Landmarks

Joshua Tree National Park is renowned for its striking landscape, where the twisted, spiky silhouettes of Joshua trees stand against a backdrop of massive rock formations and open desert skies. One of the park's most iconic sights is Hidden Valley, a secluded basin surrounded by towering rock walls that were once used by cattle rustlers to hide stolen livestock. Today, it's a popular spot for rock climbers, hikers, and those looking to explore the park's unique geology. The trail through Hidden Valley winds among massive boulders, offering a sense of discovery at every turn. As you navigate the maze of rocks, you might catch the soft rustle of a lizard darting across the sand or the distant call of a cactus wren echoing off the canyon walls.

Skull Rock, another of Joshua Tree's famous landmarks, is a natural sculpture shaped by wind and water over millennia. Its eerie, skull-like appearance—with hollowed "eye sockets"—makes it a favorite spot for visitors and photographers alike. The surrounding landscape is a playground of rounded boulders and small caves, perfect for scrambling and exploring. As the sun sets, the rocks glow with a warm, golden hue, and the play of light and shadow gives Skull Rock an almost mystical quality.

One of the most dramatic viewpoints in the park is Keys View, perched at over 5,000 feet above sea level. From this vantage point, you can gaze across the Coachella Valley, with sweeping views stretching all the way to the Salton Sea and the distant mountains of Mexico on a clear day. The wind up here is brisk, and the air carries the faint scent of desert sage. As you take in the panorama, the vastness of the desert unfolds before you—a reminder of the park's wild, untamed spirit.

The Cholla Cactus Garden, located in the transition zone between the Colorado and Mojave deserts, offers different beauty. Thousands of densely packed cholla cacti, often called "teddy bear chollas" for their deceptively fuzzy appearance, create a surreal, almost otherworldly landscape. But beware—the cactus spines are barbed and notorious for sticking to anything that brushes against them. The garden is stunning at sunrise and sunset when the cacti are backlit by the sun, their golden spines glowing like halos.

Joshua Tree is also home to Barker Dam, an oasis built by early cattle ranchers to provide water for their livestock. Today, it serves as a vital watering hole for the park's wildlife, including bighorn sheep, desert tortoises, and numerous bird species. The short, easy loop trail to Barker Dam takes you through diverse desert habitats, including Joshua trees, junipers, and pinyon pines. When the reservoir is full, the reflection of the surrounding rocks and sky on the still water creates a tranquil scene that feels miles away from the harsh desert outside.

## Hidden Gems: Lesser-Known Spots Worth Exploring

Beyond the well-trodden paths, Joshua Tree National Park harbors hidden gems that offer solitude and a deeper connection to the desert's quiet beauty. One such place is the Wonderland of Rocks, a vast and remote maze of monolithic boulders and hidden canyons. This area, accessible only by unmarked and often challenging routes, is a paradise for adventurous hikers and climbers. The boulders here are larger, and the spaces between them are narrower, creating a labyrinthine landscape where you can wander for hours without seeing another soul.

Another hidden treasure is the Lost Palms Oasis, one of the park's most remote and rewarding hikes. The 7.5-mile (12 km) round-trip trail begins at Cottonwood Spring. It leads through a rugged desert landscape, culminating in a lush oasis of fan palms tucked within a rocky canyon. The towering palms starkly contrast the surrounding desert, their green fronds offering shade and shelter to the animals that frequent the area. The solitude and the sight of water in the desert make Lost Palms Oasis feel like a true escape from the modern world.

For those seeking a quieter, less crowded viewpoint, the hike to Mastodon Peak offers panoramic vistas without the crowds found at Keys View. This moderately strenuous trail loops through rocky terrain, past the ruins of an old gold mine, and up to a small peak that rewards with sweeping views of the Eagle Mountains and the Pinto Basin. The trail's combination of history, geology, and desert scenery makes it a rewarding alternative to the more popular routes.

## Hiking Trails

Joshua Tree offers a wide range of hiking trails, each showcasing a different facet of the park's unique desert landscape.

### *Hidden Valley Nature Trail*

Length: 1 mile (1.6 km) loop
Elevation Change: Minimal
Difficulty: Easy

The Hidden Valley Nature Trail is a short, family-friendly loop that winds through one of the park's most scenic areas. Encircled by high rock walls, this sheltered valley feels like a secret world, filled with a surprising diversity of plant life that thrives in the protected environment. As you follow the sandy path, the towering boulders and unusual rock formations create an almost prehistoric ambiance. Interpretive signs along the trail provide insights into the area's flora, fauna, and history, including tales of cattle rustlers who once hid their stolen herds here.

### *Ryan Mountain Trail*

Length: 3 miles (4.8 km) round-trip
Elevation Change: 1,050 feet (320 meters)
Difficulty: Moderate

The Ryan Mountain Trail is a must for one of the best panoramic views in Joshua Tree. This steep, rocky climb leads to the summit of Ryan Mountain, where hikers are rewarded with 360-degree views of the park's iconic landscape, including the Wonderland of Rocks, Pinto Basin, and Lost Horse Valley. The trail is well-maintained but challenging, with steep switchbacks that climb relentlessly toward the summit. As you ascend, the wind picks up, and the temperature drops slightly, offering a refreshing respite from the desert heat. The summit's open, rocky expanse provides the perfect vantage point to watch the sun dip below the horizon, casting long shadows across the desert floor.

### *Lost Horse Mine Trail*

Length: 4 miles (6.4 km) round-trip
Elevation Change: 550 feet (168 meters)
Difficulty: Moderate

This trail offers a glimpse into the park's rich mining history, leading hikers to one of the best-preserved mines in Joshua Tree. The trail begins with a gentle climb through rolling hills dotted with Joshua trees and junipers, eventually reaching the ruins of the Lost Horse Mine. The old stamp mill and rusting machinery provide a tangible link to the past, evoking images of prospectors toiling under the harsh desert sun. The trail continues to a high ridge with sweeping views of the surrounding valleys—a perfect spot to pause and reflect on this land's rugged beauty and challenging history.

### *Fortynine Palms Oasis Trail*

Length: 3 miles (4.8 km) round-trip
Elevation Change: 300 feet (91 meters)
Difficulty: Moderate

This moderately challenging hike leads to a hidden oasis nestled within a rocky canyon, a lush respite from the arid landscape. The trail climbs steadily through rocky terrain, with expansive views of the surrounding desert. As you descend into the canyon, the sight of tall fan palms and the sound of trickling water come as a welcome surprise. The oasis is a haven for wildlife; lucky hikers might spot bighorn sheep, lizards, or even a desert tortoise. This trail offers a peaceful retreat, far removed from the busier parts of the park.

## Other Activities: Beyond the Trails – Experiencing Joshua Tree's Wild Side

While hiking is undoubtedly a highlight, Joshua Tree National Park offers many other activities that showcase the park's diverse landscape and unique ecosystems.

### *Rock Climbing*

Rock climbing is one of the most popular pursuits in Joshua Tree, drawing climbers worldwide to its rugged terrain. The park has over 8,000 climbing routes, with iconic spots like Hidden Valley, Intersection Rock, and Echo Cove serving as climber magnets. The park's rough granite provides excellent friction, making it a climber's paradise for bouldering, top-roping, and traditional climbing. Whether you're an experienced climber tackling challenging ascents or a beginner looking for guided lessons, Joshua Tree offers options for all skill levels. The thrill of scaling the vertical faces and reaching the summit is matched only by the breathtaking views of the surrounding desert and the unique Joshua trees swaying in the breeze.

### Stargazing

For those who prefer to keep their feet on the ground, stargazing in Joshua Tree is an unparalleled experience. The park's dark skies, far from city lights, reveal a dazzling array of stars, planets, and even the Milky Way on clear nights. After sunset, the sky transforms into a vast canvas of twinkling lights, creating a mesmerizing spectacle that invites quiet reflection and awe. Visitors can join ranger-led astronomy programs that delve into the wonders of the universe, exploring constellations and learning about celestial navigation. Alternatively, you can simply lay back on a blanket at one of the many viewpoints, such as Keys View or the Jumbo Rocks, and witness the desert sky come alive as shooting stars streak across the horizon.

### Photography

Photography enthusiasts will find endless inspiration in Joshua Tree's dramatic landscapes. The park's surreal rock formations, unique flora, and expansive desert vistas create a captivating backdrop for stunning photographs. Sunrise and sunset are the best times to capture the park's distinctive light, which casts long shadows and bathes the rocks and cacti in warm hues. Cholla Cactus Garden, with its dense clusters of cholla cacti glowing in the golden hour, is a favorite spot for photographers seeking to capture nature's artistry. Skull Rock, resembling a giant skull, offers intriguing compositions, while Arch Rock presents a natural frame for the vibrant desert sky. Whether using a professional camera or a smartphone, Joshua Tree's unique beauty inspires your creativity and leaves you with lasting memories.

## Wildlife Watching

Joshua Tree is home to diverse wildlife, making it an excellent destination for nature enthusiasts. The park's varied ecosystems support desert tortoises, bighorn sheep, and numerous bird species, including the colorful Gambel's quail and the majestic red-tailed hawk. Early mornings and late afternoons are the best times for spotting wildlife as they emerge to forage for food. Consider joining a ranger-led wildlife program to learn more about the park's inhabitants and their adaptations to the harsh desert environment. You may witness the intricate web of life that thrives in this seemingly harsh landscape with a bit of patience and a keen eye.

## Cultural Experiences

Joshua Tree has a rich cultural history that spans thousands of years, with Native American tribes such as the Cahuilla (kah-WEE-yah) and Serrano leaving their mark on the land. Participating in cultural programs can deepen your understanding of the area's history and Indigenous people's connection to the land. Look for events that highlight traditional practices, story-telling, and the significance of local plants and animals. Engaging with these cultural experiences fosters a greater appreciation for the park's heritage and the importance of preserving its stories.

## Biking

Exploring Joshua Tree on two wheels is an exhilarating way to experience the park's diverse landscapes. The park offers designated biking trails that wind through striking rock formations and lush desert vegetation. Whether you choose a leisurely ride along the paved roads or tackle the more rugged dirt paths, biking provides a unique perspective on the park's beauty. Bring your own bike or rent one in nearby towns and enjoy the thrill of exploring the desert breeze as you pedal past towering Joshua trees and sweeping vistas.

### *Picnicking*

For a more laid-back experience, picnicking in Joshua Tree lets you enjoy a meal surrounded by the park's stunning scenery. There are several designated picnic areas, including Hidden Valley and Jumbo Rocks, where you can relax and soak in the tranquility of the desert. Pack a lunch, find a shady spot, and take a moment to appreciate the unique landscape. Watching the play of light across the rocks and listening to the sounds of nature provides a perfect break from your adventures.

## Flora and Fauna: The Park's Diverse Ecosystems

Joshua Tree's unique environment supports a surprising variety of plant and animal life, thriving in the park's distinct ecosystems where the Mojave and Colorado deserts meet. The park's name-sake, the Joshua tree, is actually a species of yucca, its twisted, spiky branches creating one of the most iconic desert silhouettes in the American West. These hardy plants are perfectly adapted to the arid environment, with shallow root systems that quickly absorb rainwater and leaves that minimize water loss.

In addition to the Joshua trees, the park is home to other fascinating plant species, including the spiky cholla cacti, towering ocotillos, and delicate wildflowers that bloom in vibrant bursts of color during the spring. The high desert is characterized by pinyon pines, junipers, and scrub oak. In contrast, creosote bushes and barrel cacti dominate the lower desert areas.

Joshua Tree's wildlife is equally diverse, with species that have evolved to survive in extreme desert conditions. Bighorn sheep navigate the rocky terrain with ease, while the elusive desert tortoise spends much of its life in burrows to escape the heat. Coyotes, jackrabbits, and ground squirrels are commonly seen, and birdwatchers can spot everything from the petite phainopepla (fay-no-PEP-lah) to the impressive red-tailed hawk soaring overhead.

## Best Campgrounds and Accommodation Options

Camping in Joshua Tree is an unforgettable experience, allowing visitors to fully immerse themselves in the park's desert environment. Jumbo Rocks Campground is one of the most popular, surrounded by massive boulders that create a dramatic setting and offer opportunities for rock scrambling right from your campsite. The starry skies at night, framed by the silhouettes of Joshua trees, make for a truly magical experience.

Black Rock Campground, located on the park's northern edge, provides easy access to some of the park's best hiking and equestrian trails. With sites nestled among the Joshua trees and panoramic views of the surrounding mountains, this campground is perfect for those seeking a quieter stay.

For a more remote experience, consider the backcountry campsites scattered throughout the park. These primitive sites offer solitude and a chance to connect with nature far from the main roads. Permits are required, and campers must be prepared to pack out all waste and adhere to Leave No Trace principles.

## Documented Encounters in Joshua Tree National Park

### *The Strange Light in the Desert*

In 2018, a couple camping near Hidden Valley reported witnessing a series of unusual lights in the night sky. Sitting around the campfire, they noticed bright orbs hovering above the desert landscape. "At first, we thought it was just a reflection or possibly a drone," the woman recalled. "But the lights moved in impossible ways, darting around and hovering silently."

Intrigued and a bit unnerved, they decided to grab their camera. "We wanted to capture what we were seeing, but the lights vanished before we could get a clear shot," her partner said. The couple described the experience as mesmerizing and eerie, leaving them with a lingering sense of wonder about what they had witnessed. The event sparked conversations with fellow campers, many of whom shared similar stories of unexplained lights in the park.

### *The Phantom Hitchhiker*

In 2020, a visitor driving along the main road through Joshua Tree reported a chilling experience. While passing a remote area, he noticed a figure standing by the roadside, appearing to wave for a ride. "As I got closer, I realized it was a woman in white, but when I glanced in my rearview mirror, she had vanished," he recalled. The experience left him questioning whether he had seen a hitchhiker or something more supernatural.

*Eerie Sounds in the Desert*

In 2019, a group of friends camping in a remote area of Joshua Tree reported hearing strange, haunting sounds during the night. "It started as low growls, but then it turned into what sounded like laughter echoing through the canyons," one friend said. "We were all too scared to leave our tents." The group spent the night discussing local legends, adding an air of mystery to their adventure in the park.

## Practical Travel Tips and Planning Information

Joshua Tree is best visited in the cooler months of fall through spring when daytime temperatures are pleasant, and the desert landscape is most vibrant. Summer can be sweltering, with temperatures often exceeding 100°F (38°C), so plan accordingly with plenty of water, sun protection, and early morning or late afternoon activities.

The park's main roads, Park Boulevard and Pinto Basin Road provide access to most of the key attractions, but many areas are best explored on foot. Cell service is limited, so download maps and information ahead of time. Be mindful of the park's fragile environment—stay on designated trails, avoid touching or disturbing the cacti, and pack out all trash.

## Conclusion: Inspiring Further Exploration

Joshua Tree National Park is a place of contrasts—where the harsh desert meets delicate beauty, and solitude can be found beneath a canopy of stars. As you explore the park's rugged landscapes, towering rock formations, and iconic Joshua trees, let yourself be captivated by the quiet magic of the desert. This place inspires creativity, reflection, and a sense of adventure.

Whether you come for the climbing, the stargazing, or simply the peace of the desert, Joshua Tree offers an experience unlike any other. Embrace the stillness, respect the land, and let the desert work its timeless magic on your soul. And as you leave, consider how you can help protect this unique environment—whether through mindful visitation, supporting park conservation efforts, or simply sharing your love for Joshua Tree with others. The desert's beauty is fragile, but we can ensure it endures for generations to come.

# FOUR

# Redwood National and State Parks

## GIANTS OF THE COASTAL WILDS

 *"The redwoods are a cathedral, an inspiration for my life."*

Kevin Costner

### Introduction: The Park's History and Significance

Redwood National and State Parks, nestled along California's rugged northern coast, are home to the tallest trees on Earth. Towering up to 380 feet, the coastal redwoods stand as ancient sentinels of time, reaching skyward as they have for millennia. But beyond their sheer size, these parks hold a rich and complex history that weaves together the stories of indigenous peoples, settlers, loggers, and conservationists who fought to protect these magnificent forests.

Long before the first European explorers set foot on the Pacific shores, the land now known as Redwood National and State Parks was inhabited by Native American tribes such as the Yurok (YOO-rock), Tolowa (TAH-lo-wah), and Chilula (chih-LOO-lah. For these tribes, the redwoods were more than just trees; they were sacred beings deeply entwined with their lives spiritual and cultural fabric. The redwoods provided materials for homes, canoes, and tools. At the same time, the rivers and estuaries teemed with salmon that were essential to their diet and way of life. Ancient stories passed down through generations describe the trees as protectors and symbols of resilience, and the land itself was a living part of their identity.

The arrival of European settlers in the 19th century marked the beginning of dramatic changes for the redwoods. Drawn by the allure of gold and the promise of fertile land, settlers moved into the region in increasing numbers. The Gold Rush of the 1850s spurred a frenzy of logging, as the towering redwoods were seen as prime targets for timber. The trees were cut down at an alarming rate, felled by hand with axes and saws in an era before mechanized logging. The wood was prized for its strength and durability, and redwood lumber quickly became an essential material for building San Francisco and other burgeoning cities along the West Coast.

As the redwoods rapidly disappeared, voices began to rise in defense of these ancient giants. Early conservationists, inspired by the writings of John Muir and driven by a growing awareness of the need to protect natural landscapes, worked tirelessly to preserve what remained of the redwood forests. In 1918, the Save the Redwoods League was formed, a pioneering conservation organization dedicated to protecting the remaining stands of old-growth redwoods. Through fundraising and land purchases, the League was able to set aside key tracts of forest, laying the groundwork for the creation of California's redwood state parks in the 1920s and 1930s.

In 1968, Congress established Redwood National Park, encompassing the state parks and expanding the protected areas along the northern California coast. The park's creation was a major victory for the conservation movement, but it also came with challenges, including ongoing battles with timber companies and the need to restore areas damaged by decades of logging. Today, Redwood National and State Parks stand as a united effort between federal and state governments, working together to protect these awe-inspiring forests and the rich biodiversity they support.

The redwoods' cultural and ecological significance extends far beyond their towering trunks. The parks are home to diverse ecosystems, from fern-filled understories and coastal prairies to rocky shores where sea lions bask, and gray whales migrate offshore. Ongoing conservation efforts focus on restoring logged areas, protecting the habitats of threatened species like the marbled murrelet and the northern spotted owl, and ensuring that these ancient forests continue to thrive in the face of climate change and human impact.

## Fascinating Facts About Redwood National and State Parks

1. **Home to the Tallest Trees**: The park is famous for its coast redwoods (Sequoia sempervirens), which are the tallest trees in the world, with some reaching heights of over 370 feet (113 meters).
2. **Ancient Forests**: Some of the trees in the park are over 2,000 years old, having witnessed centuries of history.
3. **UNESCO World Heritage Site**: In 2011, Redwood National and State Parks were designated UNESCO World Heritage Sites for their exceptional natural beauty and ecological significance.

4. **Cave Systems:** The park contains several caves, including the famous Fern Canyon, known for its lush vegetation and stunning rock formations.
5. **Wildlife Habitat**: The park is home to over 400 species of vertebrates, including black bears, Roosevelt elk, and various birds, making it a vital habitat for wildlife.
6. **Endangered Species**: The park is one of the last refuges for the endangered marbled murrelet, a seabird that nests in old-growth redwoods.
7. **Unique Microclimates**: The park's coastal location creates microclimates where the weather can vary significantly over short distances, influencing the types of vegetation found.
8. **Mysterious Fog**: The coastal redwoods thrive on the fog that rolls in from the Pacific Ocean, providing moisture during dry summer.
9. **Historic Logging:** Before the parks were established, large areas of old-growth redwood forest were logged. The remaining old-growth trees are now protected, highlighting the importance of conservation efforts.
10. **Cultural Heritage**: The area has been inhabited by Indigenous peoples for thousands of years, including the Yurok, Karuk (KAH-rook), and Hupa (HOO-pah) tribes, who have a deep spiritual connection to the land.

## Key Highlights and Must-See Landmarks

Redwood National and State Parks are a place where the past and present converge in a landscape of towering trees, misty trails, and dramatic coastlines. Among the park's most iconic sites is the Tall Trees Grove, home to some of the tallest redwoods in the world, including the legendary Hyperion, which soars to an astonishing 379 feet. Accessible only by permit, the grove is a quiet sanctuary, far removed from the more frequented areas of the park. Walking among these giants feels like stepping back in time, with the soft forest floor muffling your footsteps and the canopy high above filtering sunlight into delicate beams that dance through the mist.

Fern Canyon is another must-see, a narrow, winding canyon where walls draped in lush ferns rise to 50 feet high. The canyon, which looks like something from a prehistoric era, has even been featured in movies like "Jurassic Park." As you navigate the trail, a small creek runs through the canyon's base, creating a tranquil soundtrack of trickling water. The ferns, some of which are ancient species dating back to the age of the dinosaurs, create a verdant tapestry of green that feels almost otherworldly.

Jedediah Smith Redwoods State Park, part of the larger park complex, offers some of the most pristine old-growth redwood forests in existence. The Boy Scout Tree Trail is a particular high-light, a 5.5-mile (8.8 km) round-trip hike that winds through dense towering groves, crossing small streams and climbing gentle slopes. The trail's namesake, the Boy Scout Tree, is a massive double-trunked redwood that has stood for centuries, its bark thick and gnarled with age. As you wander along the trail, the sheer size of the trees, coupled with the dappled light and the earthy scent of the forest, creates an almost spiritual atmosphere.

For those seeking coastal views, the Klamath River Overlook provides a stunning vantage point where the river meets the Pacific Ocean. On a clear day, you can see miles up and down the rugged coastline, where waves crash against rocky cliffs and seabirds soar overhead. In the spring and fall, the overlook is also a prime spot for whale watching, as gray whales migrate along the coast, often accompanied by their calves.

Another of the park's treasures is the Lady Bird Johnson Grove, dedicated to the former First Lady who championed environmental causes. The grove is easily accessible via a short loop trail. It offers a glimpse into the beauty of the redwood forest, with interpretive signs that highlight the ecological and historical significance of the area. In spring, rhododendrons bloom in vibrant pinks among the towering trunks, adding splashes of color to the lush green landscape.

## Hidden Gems: Lesser-Known Spots Worth Exploring

While the main attractions draw the crowds, Redwood National and State Parks are filled with hidden gems that offer solitude and a deeper connection to the forest. One such spot is the Stout Grove, a breathtaking stand of old-growth redwoods tucked away along the banks of the Smith River. The grove's towering trees, soft carpet of ferns, and the gentle river flow create a tranquil setting that feels far removed from the modern world. A short, easy loop trail winds through the grove, providing the perfect opportunity to soak in the grandeur of the redwoods without the hustle and bustle of larger sites.

Another hidden gem is Trillium Falls, a charming waterfall nestled within an old-growth forest near the Elk Meadow Day Use Area. The trail to the falls is a relatively easy 2.5-mile (4 km) loop that takes you through lush fern-lined paths and across wooden bridges. The falls cascade gently over moss-covered rocks, creating a serene backdrop inviting quiet contemplation. This lesser-known hike offers an intimate experience of the park's diverse landscapes, combining the redwoods' majesty with the flowing water's peaceful allure.

For a more secluded coastal experience, Enderts Beach provides a stunning stretch of shoreline away from the busier sections of the park. The beach, accessible via a short hike from the Coastal Trail, features tide pools teeming with sea life, including anemones, starfish, and crabs. The dramatic cliffs and rocky outcrops create a rugged beauty that feels wild and untamed, offering a chance to explore the park's coastal ecosystems in relative solitude.

## Hiking Trails

The hiking trails in Redwood National and State Parks offer diverse experiences, from gentle walks among towering giants to more strenuous treks with breathtaking views.

### *Prairie Creek Trail to Fern Canyon*

Length: 8 miles (12.9 km) round-trip
Elevation Change: 150 feet (46 meters)
Difficulty: Moderate

The Prairie Creek Trail is a magical journey through some of the park's most beautiful old-growth redwoods, culminating in the lush paradise of Fern Canyon. The trail begins at the Prairie Creek Visitor Center. It follows the creek through towering groves of redwoods, where sunlight filters through the canopy, creating a serene, otherworldly atmosphere. The trail is relatively flat, making it accessible to most hikers, but the real reward comes when you reach Fern Canyon. Walking through the narrow, fern-draped walls feel like entering another world, with every turn revealing a new shade of green and the soothing sound of water echoing in the canyon.

### *James Irvine Trail to Miner's Ridge Loop*

Length: 11.5 miles (18.5 km) round-trip
Elevation Change: 500 feet (152 meters)
Difficulty: Moderate

This classic loop offers one of the best all-day hikes in the park, showcasing a variety of ecosystems from towering redwoods to coastal bluffs. The trail winds through dense forests, across wooden bridges, and along ridges with glimpses of the Pacific Ocean in the distance. Along the way, you'll pass through stunning groves of ancient trees, where the forest floor is covered in ferns, and the air is filled with the earthy scent of moss and wood. The return journey on Miner's Ridge offers a slightly different perspective, with more open views and the opportunity to spot wildlife, including elk and deer.

### Tall Trees Grove Trail

Length: 4 miles (6.4 km) round-trip
Elevation Change: 800 feet (244 meters)
Difficulty: Moderate to Strenuous

One of the park's most rewarding hikes, the Tall Trees Grove Trail, requires a permit but offers an unparalleled experience among some of the world's tallest trees. The trail descends steeply into the grove, where ancient redwoods tower above you, their bark glowing in the soft light that filters through the canopy. The forest here is quiet, except for the occasional birdcall or leaves rustling in the breeze. As you make your way through the grove, you'll feel dwarfed by the sheer scale of the trees, their trunks so wide you'd need a group to wrap your arms around them. The return climb is steep but worth every step for the chance to walk among these giants.

*Boy Scout Tree Trail*

Length: 5.5 miles (8.8 km) round-trip
Elevation Change: 600 feet (183 meters)
Difficulty: Moderate

This out-and-back trail leads to the impressive Boy Scout Tree, a massive double-trunked redwood symbolizing the park's ancient forests. The trail is well-maintained and meanders through a lush, old-growth forest filled with ferns, moss-covered logs, and towering trees. The gentle ups and downs of the trail provide a moderate challenge, but the beauty of the forest makes the hike feel almost effortless. The final stretch to the Boy Scout Tree is particularly rewarding, with the tree itself standing as a testament to the enduring power of nature.

## Other Activities: Beyond the Trails – Experiencing Redwood's Coastal Wonders

While hiking among the towering redwoods is a highlight, the parks offer a variety of other activities that showcase the area's unique coastal and forested landscapes.

*Kayaking on the Smith River*

Kayaking on the Smith River provides a peaceful and immersive way to explore the park's pristine waterways. The river, with its clear, emerald-green waters, winds gracefully through towering redwood groves, creating a stunning contrast between the rich colors of the forest and the vibrant hues of the water. As you paddle gently along the river, you may encounter playful river otters frolicking in the currents. At the same time, salmon leap gracefully from the water, showcasing their strength and determination. The calm environment is perfect for beginners, allowing you to relax and appreciate the serene beauty around you. Keep your eyes peeled for various bird species, including herons and kingfishers, darting through the trees and skimming the water's surface.

### Tidepooling at Enderts Beach and Gold Bluffs Beach

For those interested in exploring the coastline, tidepooling at Enderts Beach or Gold Bluffs Beach offers a fascinating chance to discover the park's rich marine life. As you navigate the rocky outcrops during low tide, you'll be greeted by vibrant sea anemones, starfish in dazzling colors, and tiny crabs scuttling across the rocks. The rhythmic sound of waves crashing against the shore and the salty sea breeze create an immersive experience that connects you to the ocean's vitality. These beaches, often shrouded in mist, provide a moody, atmospheric backdrop that is quintessentially Pacific Northwest. During your exploration, remember to look up; you may spot a majestic gray whale migrating along the coastline, spouting water in a dramatic display of nature's wonder.

### Wildlife Watching

Wildlife watching is another popular activity in the parks, where the diversity of ecosystems creates rich habitats for various species. The Roosevelt elk, a symbol of the region, can often be seen grazing in the meadows, their impressive antlers rising majestically from their heads. The best time to observe these magnificent creatures is during the early morning or late after-noon when they are most active. Join a ranger-led program to learn about the elk's behaviors, their role in the ecosystem, and the conservation efforts in place to protect their habitat.

In addition to elk, the parks are a haven for birdwatchers. Bald eagles soar gracefully above the rivers, their keen eyesight scanning the water for fish. The parks also provide a vital nesting ground for various other bird species, making it a fantastic destination for bird enthusiasts. Bring your binoculars and a field guide to enhance your experience and consider joining a guided birdwatching tour to discover the best spots for sightings.

### *Exploring the Redwood Creek and Tall Trees Grove*

For a unique experience, consider exploring the Redwood Creek area, where you can witness the immense size of these ancient trees up close. The Tall Trees Grove, accessible via a short hike, features some of the largest and oldest redwoods in the park. The grove is a serene spot for contemplation and a place to marvel at these giants. The play of light filtering through the towering canopies creates a unique atmosphere, perfect for photography or simply soaking in the tranquility.

### *Camping Under the Stars*

Camping in the parks offers an unforgettable opportunity to experience the natural beauty of the redwoods up close. Many campgrounds are nestled among the trees, allowing you to fall asleep to the soothing sounds of rustling leaves and distant waves. Imagine sitting around a campfire, sharing stories with family and friends under a canopy of stars. The clear night skies in the parks provide a stunning backdrop for stargazing, with countless stars visible away from city lights. Consider bringing a telescope or simply lying back on a blanket to enjoy the celestial display.

*Art and Interpretation Programs*

For those interested in the cultural aspects of the park, art, and interpretation programs often provide engaging insights into the history and significance of the redwoods and their ecosystems. Workshops encourage creative expression inspired by the natural surroundings, whether through painting, photography, or writing. These programs allow visitors to connect with the landscape in a deeper way, fostering a greater appreciation for the beauty and importance of preserving these ancient trees.

## Flora and Fauna: The Park's Diverse Ecosystems

The diverse ecosystems of Redwood National and State Parks are home to a rich array of plant and animal life. The towering redwoods, some of which are over 2,000 years old, dominate the landscape, creating a lush canopy that supports a unique understory of ferns, mosses, and wildflowers. The forests are filled with towering Douglas firs, Sitka spruce, and western hemlock, adding to the park's lush, green ambiance.

The park's coastal prairies and river valleys provide important habitats for various wildlife. Roosevelt elk, the largest land mammals in the park, can often be seen grazing in the open meadows, their massive antlers a striking sight against the green landscape. The rivers and streams that flow through the parks are home to salmon, steelhead, and other native fish species, and the park's birdlife includes everything from the tiny chestnut-backed chickadee to the majestic bald eagle.

The park's coastal areas are equally rich in biodiversity, with rocky shores that support tidepool creatures, seabirds, and marine mammals. Harbor seals and sea lions can often be spotted lounging on the rocks. At the same time, gray whales migrate offshore between feeding and breeding grounds. The interconnectedness of these ecosystems highlights the importance of protecting the park's diverse habitats and the species that depend on them.

## Best Campgrounds and Accommodation Options

Camping in Redwood National and State Parks offers a unique opportunity to sleep under the towering giants and wake up to the sounds of the forest. Jedediah Smith Campground, located along the banks of the Smith River, is a favorite for its proximity to old-growth redwoods and easy access to the park's best hiking trails. The sites are nestled among the trees, providing a serene, secluded camping experience.

Gold Bluffs Beach Campground, set along the park's rugged coastline, offers a different kind of adventure. With campsites right on the sand and stunning views of the ocean, falling asleep to the sound of crashing waves and waking up to misty coastal mornings is an experience unlike any other. The campground also provides easy access to Fern Canyon, one of the park's most popular attractions.

For those seeking a more rustic experience, backcountry camping is available with a permit. It allows you to truly immerse yourself in the park's wilderness. Backcountry sites like the ones along the Redwood Creek Trail provide solitude and the chance to camp among ancient redwoods, far from the crowds.

## Documented Encounters in Redwood National Park

### *The Vanishing Hiker*

In the summer of 2017, a hiker named Jessica embarked on a solo journey through the lush trails of Fern Canyon in Redwood National Park. Known for its towering redwoods and rich biodiversity, the area was a favorite among nature enthusiasts. As Jessica hiked deeper into the canyon, she was captivated by the vibrant green ferns and the sound of water trickling nearby.

While traversing a narrow path that hugged the canyon walls, Jessica noticed a man ahead of her, seemingly lost and disoriented. He appeared to be in his mid-thirties, wearing a tattered backpack and a look of confusion on his face. Concerned, Jessica quickened her pace to offer assistance. As she approached, she asked if he needed help, but the man only muttered something unintelligible, his eyes darting nervously around.

Jessica suggested they retrace their steps together, but he seemed hesitant as if drawn to venture deeper into the woods. After a brief conversation, she turned away to grab her water bottle, intending to guide him back to the main trail. When she turned back just moments later, the man had vanished.

Feeling unsettled, Jessica scanned the surrounding area, calling out to him, but there was no response. The forest around her was eerily silent, and she felt a chill creep up her spine. After searching for several minutes, she decided it was best to return to the main path and alert park rangers about the encounter. When she reported the incident, the rangers informed her that they had received similar reports of people encountering lost hikers in that area—some of whom had never been found.

Jessica left the park that day with a mix of intrigue and unease. The experience lingered in her mind long after she returned home, prompting her to wonder about the stories hidden within the ancient trees and whether the man she had encountered was just another visitor—or something more mysterious.

### *The Echoing Laughter*

A family camping near the Klamath River reported hearing children's laughter echoing through the trees late one evening. They described it as a joyful sound that seemed to come from nowhere and everywhere at once. When they investigated, they found no one else in the vicinity. The laughter continued sporadically throughout the night, creating an enchanting and slightly unsettling atmosphere.

## Practical Travel Tips and Planning Information

Redwood National and State Parks are best visited in the spring and fall when the weather is mild, and the park's trails are less crowded. Summer can bring fog along the coast, adding a moody atmosphere to the forest. At the same time, winter storms can create dramatic coastal scenes but may also cause trail closures. Be sure to pack layers, as temperatures can vary significantly between the forest and the coast.

The parks are spread out along a 50-mile stretch of coastline, so plan your route in advance to make the most of your visit. The Newton B. Drury Scenic Parkway and Howland Hill Road offer some of the best drives through the redwoods, with opportunities to stop and explore along the way. Remember to bring plenty of water, as some of the trails can be long and remote, and always stay on designated paths to protect the delicate forest floor.

## Conclusion: Inspiring Further Exploration

Redwood National and State Parks are more than just a collection of towering trees; they are a living testament to the natural world's beauty, resilience, and interconnectedness. Walking among the ancient giants, listening to the wind rustling through the canopy, and feeling the cool mist on your face, you are part of a story that spans millennia. Let the majesty of the redwoods inspire you to explore, protect, and cherish the wild places that still exist in our world.

Whether standing beneath the tallest trees on Earth, exploring a fern-filled canyon, or gazing out over the rugged Pacific coast, Redwood National and State Parks invite you to slow down, look up, and reconnect with nature. These forests have stood the test of time. They will continue to stand for generations to come with continued conservation efforts. Let the redwoods remind you of the power of nature and the importance of protecting these ancient landscapes for the future.

# FIVE

# Mount Rainier National Park

## A MAJESTIC MOUNTAIN OF FIRE AND ICE

*"Mount Rainier is a volcano that is more than a mountain; it is a symbol of the wild spirit of the Pacific Northwest."*

Tim McNulty

### Introduction: The Park's History and Significance

Rising to an imposing 14,411 feet, Mount Rainier dominates the skyline of the Pacific Northwest, its glaciated peak often shrouded in a veil of clouds. As the most prominent mountain in the contiguous United States, this active stratovolcano is not just a geographical marvel but a cultural icon and a testament to the forces that shape our world. The park's history is rich with stories of Native American tribes, pioneering climbers, and conservationists who recognized the need to protect its pristine beauty.

For thousands of years, Mount Rainier was revered by the indigenous peoples of the region, including the Puyallup (pew-AL-up), Nisqually (niss-KWAH-lee), and Yakama (YAK-uh-mah) tribes, who knew it by names like Tahoma or Tacoma, meaning "the mountain that was God." The mountain was a powerful presence to them, deeply intertwined with their spiritual beliefs and daily lives. They hunted, gathered, and traveled through the surrounding forests and meadows, respecting the mountain as a sacred place of great importance. Oral traditions speak of spirits inhabiting the summit and cautionary tales of those who ventured too close.

The first recorded sighting of Mount Rainier by Europeans occurred in 1792 when Captain George Vancouver, exploring the waters of Puget Sound, named the mountain after his friend, Rear Admiral Peter Rainier. However, in the mid-19th century, Mount Rainier began to capture the attention of settlers and adventurers. Early explorers like Hazard Stevens and Philemon Beecher Van Trump made the first successful summit in 1870, enduring grueling conditions to reach the top. Their accounts of the climb, filled with tales of crevasses, snowfields, and the thrilling view from the summit, sparked a wave of interest in mountaineering that continues to this day.

As more people were drawn to the mountain's rugged beauty, the need to protect Mount Rainier's delicate ecosystems became apparent. In 1899, Mount Rainier National Park was established, becoming America's fifth national park and the first to be created from an active volcano. The park's establishment marked a significant victory for the conservation movement, ensuring the preservation of its diverse landscapes, from ancient forests and alpine meadows to vast glaciers and volcanic peaks.

Mount Rainier's role in conservation extends beyond its scenic value. The park's diverse ecosystems support a wide range of plant and animal species, many of which are found nowhere else. Conservation efforts today focus on preserving the park's unique habitats, monitoring the glaciers that cover the mountain, and protecting the park's natural and cultural resources from the impacts of climate change and increased visitation. The mountain's glaciers, which feed five major river systems, are vital to the region's water supply, and their retreat offers a stark reminder of the ongoing challenges posed by a warming climate.

Mount Rainier's significance is not just ecological but also cultural. The park has long been a place of inspiration, drawing artists, writers, and outdoor enthusiasts captivated by its beauty and power. Mount Rainier stands as a symbol of the enduring spirit of the Pacific Northwest, from the wildflower-strewn meadows of Paradise to the towering summit. In this place, nature's raw power and delicate beauty coexist.

## Fascinating Facts About Mount Rainier National Park

1. **Active Volcano**: Mount Rainier is an active stratovolcano and the highest peak in the Cascade Range, standing at 14,411 feet (4,392 meters).
2. **Glacial Wonderland**: The park is home to 26 major glaciers, which account for about 40% of the mountain's area, making it one of the most glaciated peaks in the contiguous United States.
3. **Historic Structures**: The park features historic structures, including the 1916 Paradise Inn, which showcases rustic architecture and serves as a visitor hub.

1. **First National Park**: Established in 1899, Mount Rainier was the fifth national park in the United States and the first to be designated in Washington.
2. **Volcanic History**: Mount Rainier last erupted in 1894, and while it is currently considered dormant, geologists continue to monitor the volcano for signs of activity.
3. **Unique Weather Patterns**: Mount Rainier receives an average of 100 to 150 inches of rainfall annually, contributing to its lush vegetation and creating a unique microclimate.
4. **Historic Trails**: The park features over 260 miles of hiking trails, including the famous Wonderland Trail, which circumnavigates the mountain.
5. **Hydrothermal Features**: The park has several hydrothermal features, including fumaroles, hot springs, and boiling mud pots, particularly in the active areas surrounding the mountain.
6. **First Female Ranger**: In 1917, Margaret "Maggie" McGowan became the first female ranger in the National Park Service, serving at Mount Rainier.
7. **Presidential Designation**: In 1988, Mount Rainier was designated a National Historic Landmark District for its historical and architectural significance.

## Key Highlights and Must-See Landmarks

Mount Rainier National Park is a treasure trove of natural wonders, with each corner offering a new vista or experience that showcases the park's dramatic landscape. One of the most iconic areas of the park is Paradise, a subalpine region renowned for its stunning wildflower displays, sweeping views, and access to some of the park's best trails. In the summer, the meadows of Paradise burst into color with lupines, paintbrush, and avalanche lilies, creating a vibrant mosaic against the backdrop of Mount Rainier's snowy peak. The scent of wildflowers mingles with the crisp mountain air, and the sound of marmots whistling from rocky outcrops adds to the sense of being in a truly wild place.

Nearby, the historic Paradise Inn, built in 1916, offers a glimpse into the park's early days as a destination for adventurers and nature lovers. The lodge, constructed from massive timbers and native stone, exudes rustic charm, with cozy fireplaces and large windows that frame mountain views. A short walk from the inn, the Skyline Trail leads to spectacular viewpoints, including Panorama Point, where, on a clear day, you can see as far as Mount Adams, Mount Hood, and even Mount St. Helens.

The Sunrise area, located on the northeastern side of the park, is the highest point accessible by car and offers some of the most breathtaking views of Mount Rainier. As you ascend the winding road to Sunrise, the landscape transitions from dense forest to open alpine meadows, with sweeping vistas of the mountain's glaciated slopes and the Emmons Glacier, the largest glacier in the contiguous United States. The Sunrise Visitor Center provides exhibits on the park's geology and wildlife, and the nearby trails offer opportunities to explore the park's alpine environment, where mountain goats and black bears are often spotted.

For those looking closer at the park's volcanic features, the Carbon River and Mowich Lake areas offer a rugged, less-traveled side of Mount Rainier. The Carbon Glacier, one of the lowest elevation glaciers in the contiguous United States, can be reached via a scenic hike through old-growth forest, where ancient trees tower overhead and rushing water fills the air. The nearby Tolmie Peak Lookout provides a panoramic view of Mowich Lake, the surrounding forests, and Mount Rainier's imposing summit, reflecting on the water's surface like a shimmering mirror.

One of the park's most unique geological features is the Wonderland Trail, a 93-mile (150 km) loop that circumnavigates the entire mountain. This challenging trail offers intrepid hikers the chance to experience the full range of Mount Rainier's landscapes, from dense forests and glacial rivers to alpine meadows and volcanic ridges. Completing the Wonderland Trail is a bucket-list achievement for many, offering a journey through some of the most diverse and dramatic scenery in the Pacific Northwest.

## Hidden Gems: Lesser-Known Spots Worth Exploring

While Mount Rainier's popular spots draw crowds, the park also offers quieter, lesser-known areas that provide a more intimate connection to the mountain's rugged beauty. One such hidden gem is the Ohanapecosh (oh-HAH-nuh-peh-kosh) area, located on the park's southeastern edge. Known for its lush old-growth forests and crystal-clear rivers, Ohanapecosh feels like a hidden paradise, with towering Douglas firs and western red cedars creating a dense canopy overhead. The Grove of the Patriarchs, a short, easy hike from the Ohanapecosh Visitor Center, leads to a grove of ancient trees, some over 1,000 years old, protected by the surrounding river for centuries.

For a more remote and challenging adventure, the Spray Park Trail offers a rewarding journey through wildflower meadows, cascading waterfalls, and stunning views of Mount Rainier's northern face. This trail, less crowded than the popular Paradise and Sunrise areas, takes hikers through a varied landscape that feels truly wild. The final ascent to Spray Park reveals panoramic vistas of Mount Rainier and the surrounding peaks, with the roar of nearby Spray Falls providing a dramatic soundtrack.

Another hidden treasure is the Carbon River Rainforest, an area unlike any other in the park. The rainforest, characterized by lush ferns, moss-covered trees, and the sound of rain dripping from the canopy, feels more like the Olympic Peninsula than Mount Rainier. The Carbon River Road, which is now closed to vehicles due to flood damage, has been converted into a hiking and biking trail, offering a peaceful journey through this unique ecosystem. The nearby Green Lake Trail, a short but steep hike, leads to a serene alpine lake nestled among towering evergreens, offering solitude and a sense of discovery.

## Hiking Trails

Mount Rainier National Park is a hiker's Paradise, offering trails that range from leisurely strolls to challenging summit climbs. Each trail provides a different perspective on the mountain's diverse landscapes.

### *Skyline Trail to Panorama Point*

Length: 5.5 miles (8.9 km) loop
Elevation Change: 1,700 feet (518 meters)
Difficulty: Moderate

The Skyline Trail, one of the most popular hikes in the park, offers a stunning journey through the wildflower meadows of Paradise, with panoramic views of Mount Rainier and the surrounding peaks. The trail begins near the Paradise Visitor Center and ascends through lush meadows filled with lupines, paintbrush, and glacier lilies. As you climb higher, the views reveal the majesty of Mount Rainier's summit and the Nisqually Glacier. At Panorama Point, the trail's high point, the view stretches for miles, encompassing distant peaks and the rolling landscape of the Cascade Range. The return loop takes you past Myrtle Falls, where water cascades over a rocky ledge framed by vibrant wildflowers.

## *Burroughs Mountain Trail*

Length: 9 miles (14.5 km) round-trip
Elevation Change: 2,500 feet (762 meters)
Difficulty: Strenuous

For those seeking a more challenging hike, the Burroughs Mountain Trail offers some of the best up-close views of Mount Rainier's glaciers and rocky slopes. Starting from the Sunrise area, the trail climbs steadily through alpine meadows and rocky outcrops, each revealing a more dramatic view of the mountain. The trail's three summits—First, Second, and Third Burroughs—provide progressively closer perspectives on Rainier's Emmons Glacier, with the final summit feeling almost within reach of the icy slopes. The rugged terrain and sweeping vistas make this hike a favorite among seasoned hikers.

## *Tolmie Peak Lookout Trail*

Length: 5.6 miles (9 km) round-trip
Elevation Change: 1,100 feet (335 meters)
Difficulty: Moderate

This scenic trail begins at Mowich Lake and climbs through dense forest past Eunice Lake to the historic Tolmie Peak Fire Lookout. The trail is moderately challenging, with a steep ascent to the lookout, but the reward is well worth the effort. From the lookout, you'll enjoy panoramic views of Mount Rainier, the surrounding Cascade peaks, and the shimmering waters of Mowich Lake far below. On clear days, the mountain seems to float above the landscape, its glaciers glowing in the sunlight.

*Comet Falls Trail*

Length: 3.8 miles (6.1 km) round-trip
Elevation Change: 1,250 feet (381 meters)
Difficulty: Moderate

The Comet Falls Trail offers a stunning journey through forested slopes and along cascading streams, culminating at one of the park's most impressive waterfalls. The trail begins with a steady climb through old-growth forest, crossing footbridges over rushing creeks and passing smaller waterfalls. As you approach Comet Falls, the sound of crashing water grows louder, and soon, you're greeted by the sight of a 320-foot waterfall plummeting down a rocky cliff. The mist from the falls creates rainbows in the sunlight, adding to the magical atmosphere of the hike.

## Other Activities: Beyond the Trails – Experiencing Mount Rainier's Alpine Playground

While hiking is undoubtedly a highlight, Mount Rainier National Park offers many activities that showcase the park's diverse landscapes and exhilarating outdoor experiences.

*Mountaineering and Climbing*

For those seeking an adrenaline rush, mountaineering and climbing are popular pursuits, with the Disappointment Cleaver and Emmons Glacier routes offering challenging ascents to the summit of Mount Rainier. The park is renowned as one of North America's premier climbing destinations, attracting experienced climbers eager to test their skills against the mountain's formidable terrain. Guided climbs are available for those who want to experience the thrill of reaching the summit while learning essential techniques from expert guides. Climbers navigate through snowfields, crevasses, and icy slopes, where each step brings them closer to the breathtaking views at the top. Standing at 14,411 feet, the sense of accomplishment is palpable as climbers gaze out over the vast expanse of the Cascade Range and beyond.

### Winter Wonderland Activities

Mount Rainier transforms into a snowy wonderland perfect for snowshoeing, cross-country skiing, and sledding in winter. The Paradise area becomes a hub for winter activities, featuring marked snowshoe routes and groomed ski trails that offer stunning views of the mountain's snow-covered slopes. Families and adventurers flock to this winter playground, where the landscape glistens under a blanket of fresh snow. The National Park Service offers guided snowshoe walks during winter, providing a fun and educational way to explore the park's snowy landscapes. Rangers share insights about the park's ecology and history while leading participants through the serene, snow-blanketed trails, creating an unforgettable experience.

### Wildlife Watching

Mount Rainier is home to diverse wildlife, making it an excellent destination for nature enthusiasts. Visitors may spot black bears, elk, mountain goats, and various bird species, including the elusive peregrine falcon. Early mornings and late afternoons are the best times for wildlife watching, as many animals are more active during these cooler hours. Consider joining a ranger-led wildlife program to learn about the behaviors and habitats of these fascinating creatures. Observing wildlife in their natural environment adds an extra layer of excitement to your visit.

## Photography

Photography is another beloved activity at Mount Rainier, with countless opportunities to capture the beauty of the park's diverse environments. Sunrise and sunset are particularly great times when the light bathes the mountain in pink, orange, and purple hues. The Reflection Lakes area, located along Stevens Canyon Road, provides iconic photo opportunities, with Mount Rainier perfectly mirrored in the calm waters. Photographers can also explore vibrant wildflower meadows in the summer, where fields of lupines and Indian paintbrush create a stunning scene against the backdrop of the towering mountain. Each season offers unique photographic opportunities, inviting amateur and professional photographers to capture the park's changing beauty.

## Cultural and Educational Programs

Mount Rainier National Park offers various cultural and educational programs designed to deepen visitors' understanding of the park's history and natural environment. Attend ranger-led talks and demonstrations that cover topics such as the region's Indigenous cultures, the mountain's geology, and conservation efforts. These programs provide an engaging way to learn about the park's significance and the delicate balance of its ecosystems. Many visitors find that participating in these programs enriches their experience, fostering a greater appreciation for the natural world.

## Camping Under the Stars

Camping in Mount Rainier National Park allows you to fully immerse yourself in the wilderness's stunning landscapes and tranquil beauty. The park offers several campgrounds, each providing unique opportunities to connect with nature. Imagine setting up your tent amidst towering trees, with the sounds of nature surrounding you. The starry sky comes alive as night falls, providing a perfect backdrop for stargazing. The park's remote location and elevation mean you can often see constellations and celestial events with breathtaking clarity. Sharing stories around the campfire while gazing up at the Milky Way is a quintessential experience for many visitors.

### Fishing

For those seeking a more tranquil experience, fishing in Mount Rainier's pristine rivers and lakes can be a relaxing way to connect with the outdoors. The park is home to several fishing spots, including the pristine waters of the Nisqually River and the lakes within the park boundaries. Anglers can cast their lines for rainbow trout, cutthroat trout, and brook trout, enjoying the serenity of nature while waiting for a bite. Check the park's fishing regulations and obtain any necessary permits before you start. Practice catch-and-release to help preserve the park's aquatic ecosystems.

## Flora and Fauna: The Park's Diverse Ecosystems

Mount Rainier's diverse ecosystems, ranging from lowland forests to alpine tundra, support a rich variety of plant and animal life. The park is famous for its wildflower meadows, which burst into bloom during the summer months, creating a vibrant carpet of color against the backdrop of the snow-capped peak. Species like lupines, avalanche lilies, and Indian paintbrush thrive in the subalpine meadows, attracting pollinators such as bees and butterflies.

The park's forests, dominated by towering Douglas firs, western hemlocks, and Alaska yellow cedars, provide habitat for wildlife, including black bears, elk, and mountain lions. Birdwatchers can spot species like the Clark's nutcracker, mountain bluebird, and the elusive northern spotted owl. The rivers and streams that flow from the mountain's glaciers are home to native fish species, including rainbow and cutthroat trout.

Mount Rainier's high-altitude zones are characterized by rugged terrain and sparse vegetation. Still, they are home to hardy species like the American pika, mountain goats, and the elusive hoary marmot. These animals have adapted to survive in the harsh conditions of the alpine environment, enduring cold temperatures and thin air.

## Best Campgrounds and Accommodation Options

Camping in Mount Rainier National Park offers a chance to sleep under the stars and wake up to the sound of birdsong and rushing water. Cougar Rock Campground, located near Paradise, is a favorite for its proximity to the park's main attractions and scenic setting along the Nisqually River. The sites are nestled among towering trees, providing shade and a sense of seclusion.

For a more remote experience, the White River Campground near Sunrise offers stunning views of the surrounding peaks and easy access to some of the park's best hiking trails. The sites are more rustic, but the reward is a peaceful setting with panoramic mountain views.

Backcountry camping is also available for those exploring the park's wilderness areas. Permits are required, and campers should be prepared for changing weather conditions and practice Leave No Trace principles. Popular backcountry sites include those along the Wonderland Trail, offering solitude and the chance to camp in the shadow of Mount Rainier.

## Mysterious Encounters: Unexplained Sightings at Mount Rainier National Park

### *The Mysterious Light Phenomenon*

In the summer of 1947, campers reported seeing strange lights near Mount Rainier. They described the lights as bright orbs that danced across the sky, changing colors and moving in unexplainable patterns. Witnesses included experienced outdoorsmen familiar with the area and the natural phenomena that could occur.

One camper noted, "We were just sitting around the campfire when these lights appeared above the mountain. At first, we thought they were just distant stars, but they began to move and pulse in a way I had never seen before." The lights reportedly hovered and darted back and forth before disappearing entirely, leaving the campers in awe and confusion.

The sightings gained attention from local media, and even the U.S. Air Force investigated the reports, but no explanation was ever given. The incident remains one of the many mysterious encounters tied to Mount Rainier, fueling speculation about unidentified aerial phenomena in the region.

### *The Vanishing Hiker*

In 1981, a hiker disappeared in the park under mysterious circumstances. Despite extensive search efforts, he was never found. Months later, some park visitors reported seeing a figure resembling the missing hiker wandering near the trails late at night, only to vanish when approached. This account has added to the park's lore about the unexplained disappearances that sometimes occur in remote areas.

### The Phantom Music

Several visitors have reported hearing faint, melodic music echoing through the valleys near the Nisqually Glacier. These sounds, described as ethereal and almost haunting, have been reported at dusk or dawn. Some believe the music is linked to the spirits of early mountaineers or Native American folklore, as it tends to resonate near ancient trails and sacred sites.

## Practical Travel Tips and Planning Information

Mount Rainier is best visited from late June to September when the weather is mild, and the park's wildflower meadows are in full bloom. Early mornings and weekdays are the best times to visit to avoid crowds, especially in popular areas like Paradise and Sunrise. Be prepared for changing weather conditions, as the mountain's climate can be unpredictable, with rain, snow, and fog possible at any time.

Pack layers, sturdy hiking boots, and plenty of water, as many of the park's trails are steep and exposed. The park's main roads, including the Paradise and Sunrise access roads, offer stunning drives with numerous pullouts for scenic views. Check road conditions before your trip, as some roads may be closed due to snow or maintenance.

Mount Rainier's rugged terrain and wildlife require a few safety considerations. Stay on marked trails, know your surroundings, and carry bear spray when hiking in remote areas. If you plan to summit the mountain, ensure you're adequately equipped and consider joining a guided climb for added safety.

## Conclusion: Inspiring Further Exploration

Mount Rainier National Park is a place of breathtaking beauty and boundless adventure, where the power of nature is on full display. As you explore its towering peaks, lush forests, and vibrant meadows, take a moment to appreciate the forces that have shaped this landscape over millennia. From the thundering waterfalls and ancient glaciers to the quiet moments spent gazing at the mountain's reflection, Mount Rainier invites you to reconnect with the natural world.

Whether you're summiting the peak, exploring the wildflower meadows, or simply sitting quietly beside an alpine lake, Mount Rainier offers an experience that stays with you long after you've left. Let the mountain's majesty inspire you to explore further, protect these wild places, and cherish the moments of awe that only nature can provide. The mountain stands as a reminder of our connection to the earth and the importance of preserving its beauty for future generations.

# Make a Difference With Your Review

## PACIFIC WONDERS: EXPLORING THE NATIONAL PARKS

*"The clearest way into the Universe is through a forest wilderness."*

John Muir

Exploring the beauty of our national parks brings a deeper appreciation for the world around us. If sharing this journey can inspire others to step into nature's wonders, then I'm all in!

To make that happen, I have a question for you...

Would you help someone you've never met, even if you never got credit for it?

Who is this person, you ask? They're like you. They dream of hiking among ancient redwoods, marveling at volcanic craters, and feeling the mist of ocean waves in untouched coastal preserves —but they're not sure where to begin.

Our mission is to make *Pacific Wonders* accessible to everyone who dreams of exploring these incredible places. Every page, every story, is a step toward that goal. And the best way to make it happen is by reaching... well... everyone. This is where you come in. Most people do, in fact, judge a book by its cover (and its reviews). So, here's my ask, on behalf of all the people you've never met who are searching for their next adventure:

**Please help that person discover the magic of the Pacific parks by leaving this book a review.**

Your gift costs no money and takes less than sixty seconds, but it can ignite a love for the wild places that change lives. Your review could help...

- ...one more person find the inspiration to set out on their first hike
- ...one more adventurer discover a hidden gem within these parks
- ...one more nature lover reconnect with the beauty around them
- ...a fellow explorer find the right guide for their next outdoor journey

To get that "feel-good" feeling and help this person for real, all you have to do is... and it takes less than sixty seconds... leave a review. Simply scan the QR code below to leave your review:

If you feel good about helping a fellow nature enthusiast discover their next great adventure, you are my kind of person. Welcome to the club. You're one of us.

I'm that much more excited to guide you through the wonders of these parks in the pages that follow. I hope they bring you as much joy as they brought me.

Thank you from the bottom of my heart. Now, back to our regularly scheduled adventure.

**Your fellow explorer,**
- Everett Wilder

SIX

# Olympic National Park

## A TAPESTRY OF MOUNTAINS, FORESTS, AND COASTLINES

*"Olympic National Park is a treasure of the Pacific Northwest, a place where the mountains meet the sea and the wild spirit of nature reigns supreme."*

Unknown

### Introduction: The Park's History and Significance

Olympic National Park is a land of contrasts and diversity, where lush temperate rainforests, rugged mountain peaks, and wild, windswept coastlines coexist within a single, extraordinary landscape. Spanning nearly a million acres on Washington's Olympic Peninsula, the park is a testament to the power of nature's forces, shaped by ancient glaciers, volcanic activity, and relentless ocean waves. Its history is as rich and varied as its ecosystems, woven with the stories of indigenous tribes, explorers, and conservationists who have long recognized the park's unique beauty and importance.

For thousands of years, the Olympic Peninsula was home to Native American tribes, including the Hoh (rhymes with "go"), Quinault (kwin-AWLT), Quileute (KWIL-ee-oot), and Makah (muh-KAW), who lived in harmony with the land, relying on its abundant resources for their sustenance and spiritual practices. The forests, rivers, and coastlines were not just sources of food and shelter, but sacred spaces deeply intertwined with the tribes' cultural heritage. The towering Sitka spruce and western red cedar were used to build longhouses and carve canoes, while the rivers teemed with salmon that were integral to their diet and way of life. The tribes maintain a strong connection to the land, practicing traditional fishing, hunting, and gathering within the park.

The first European explorers arrived in the late 18th century, drawn by tales of wild and uncharted land. In 1788, British Captain John Meares was among the first to sail along the peninsula's rugged coast, followed by the Lewis and Clark expedition in the early 1800s, which documented the region's vast natural wealth. By the late 19th century, settlers had begun to penetrate the dense forests of the Olympic Mountains, seeking timber, minerals, and land for homesteads. The logging industry quickly took hold, and the ancient trees of the Olympic rainforest became prime targets for harvest, with little thought given to the long-term impact on the landscape.

As the pace of logging accelerated, early conservationists began to sound the alarm, recognizing the need to protect the peninsula's unique ecosystems before they were lost forever. Among them was John Muir, whose passionate advocacy for wilderness preservation helped galvanize public support for creating national parks nationwide. In 1909, President Theodore Roosevelt designated the core of the Olympic Mountains as Mount Olympus National Monument, a crucial first step in protecting the area's fragile environment.

However, Olympic National Park wasn't officially established until 1938, thanks to the efforts of President Franklin D. Roosevelt, who was struck by the park's untamed beauty during a visit. The park's creation marked a significant victory for the conservation movement, safeguarding a vast expanse of wilderness that included the rugged mountains, lush rainforests, and wild coastlines that make Olympic National Park so unique.

Today, the park is recognized as a UNESCO World Heritage Site and Biosphere Reserve, highlighting its global significance as one of the world's most diverse and pristine ecosystems. Ongoing conservation efforts focus on protecting the park's delicate balance, from restoring salmon habitats and removing invasive species to managing the impacts of climate change and increasing visitation. The park's rich cultural and ecological legacy continues to inspire visitors, offering a glimpse into the wild, untamed beauty of the Pacific Northwest.

## Fascinating Facts About Olympic National Park

1. **Diverse Ecosystems**: Olympic National Park is home to three distinct ecosystems: temperate rainforests, alpine regions, and rugged coastline.
2. **Hoh Rainforest**: It receives over 140 inches of rain yearly, making it one of the wettest places in the United States.
3. **Mount Olympus**: The park's highest peak, Mount Olympus, rises to 7,965 feet and is a popular destination for mountaineers.
4. **Rich Biodiversity**: Olympic National Park boasts over 1,400 species of vascular plants, highlighting its biodiversity.

1. **Ancient Trees:** The park features some of the oldest trees in the country, with some western red cedars over 1,000 years old.
2. **Strait of Juan de Fuca**: The park's coastline borders the Strait of Juan de Fuca, which separates the U.S. from Canada.
3. **Historic Lighthouses**: The park has several historic lighthouses, including the iconic Cape Flattery Lighthouse.
4. **Lake Crescent**: This deep blue lake is about 624 feet deep and was formed by glacial activity thousands of years ago.
5. **Native American Heritage**: The park is rich in Native American history, with several tribes having lived in the area for thousands of years.
6. **Elwha River Restoration**: Removing two dams on the Elwha River has allowed salmon to return to their historic spawning grounds.

## Key Highlights and Must-See Landmarks

Olympic National Park's diverse landscapes are a kaleidoscope of natural beauty, where each area offers a distinct and unforgettable experience. One of the park's most iconic regions is the Hoh Rainforest, a lush, green wonderland where moss-draped trees and fern-filled undergrowth create a scene straight out of a fairy tale. The Hoh Rainforest receives an astounding 12 to 14 feet of rain each year, nurturing one of the world's most vibrant temperate rainforests. Walking along the Hall of Mosses Trail, the air is thick with damp earth and cedar scent. The silence is broken only by the soft patter of raindrops and the occasional call of a spotted owl hidden high in the canopy.

Rising above the rainforests and valleys, the Olympic Mountains form the rugged heart of the park, crowned by the snow-covered summit of Mount Olympus, which reaches 7,980 feet. The Hurricane Ridge area offers some of the most accessible and breathtaking views of these mountains, with sweeping vistas of jagged peaks, alpine meadows, and distant glaciers. On clear days, you can see as far as Vancouver Island and the San Juan Islands, with the Strait of Juan de Fuca shimmering in the distance. In summer, the meadows around Hurricane Ridge burst into bloom with wildflowers, painting the landscape in vibrant purple, yellow, and red hues.

Olympic's coastline is another highlight, stretching for 73 miles along the wild Pacific Ocean. Here, rugged sea stacks rise from the crashing waves, tide pools teem with colorful marine life, and sandy beaches give way to windswept headlands. Rialto Beach is one of the park's most popular coastal spots, where the dramatic sea stacks and driftwood-strewn shore create a striking, almost surreal scene. At low tide, the beach reveals a hidden world of tide pools filled with sea anemones, starfish, and crabs, each one a tiny universe of color and life.

Further south, the beaches of Kalaloch offer a quieter coastal expe-rience, with wide, sandy expanses perfect for beachcombing, picnicking, and watching the sunset over the ocean. The nearby Tree of Life, a gnarled Sitka spruce that clings precariously to the edge of a bluff, is a testament to nature's resilience. Its exposed roots hang in midair above an eroded cliff. The sight of this tree, seemingly defying gravity and the forces of time, is both humbling and inspiring.

Another must-see is Lake Crescent, a glacially carved lake known for its deep blue waters and stunning mountain backdrop. The lake's clarity is legendary, with visibility reaching depths over 60 feet. Surrounded by forested slopes, the lake offers opportunities for kayaking, swimming, and hiking. The nearby Marymere Falls

Trail provides a short, scenic walk to a picturesque waterfall that cascades into a fern-lined grotto.

## Hidden Gems: Lesser-Known Spots Worth Exploring

While Olympic National Park's main attractions draw visitors from around the world, the park is also home to hidden gems that offer quieter, more intimate experiences of its diverse landscapes. One such spot is Sol Duc Hot Springs. In this natural oasis, geothermal waters bubble up from deep within the earth, offering a soothing retreat in the heart of the forest. The hot springs, long used by Native American tribes for their healing properties, are now part of a rustic resort that allows visitors to soak in the mineral-rich waters, surrounded by towering trees and the sound of the nearby river.

For those seeking solitude, the Enchanted Valley is a remote, verdant valley accessible only by a challenging hike along the Quinault River. Known as the "Valley of 10,000 Waterfalls," this secluded area is filled with cascading waterfalls that tumble down the sheer cliffs of the valley walls, creating a symphony of rushing water. The trail to the Enchanted Valley winds through ancient forests, crossing rivers and meadows where elk and black bears are often seen. Camping in this secluded valley, surrounded by the sounds of waterfalls and wildlife, feels like stepping into another world.

The Staircase area, located in the park's southeastern corner, offers a rugged and less-traveled experience, with trails that wind through old-growth forests along the Skokomish River. The Staircase Rapids Loop is a particularly scenic hike, with the trail following the rushing river as it tumbles over boulders and through moss-covered gorges. The dense forest, filled with towering Douglas firs and western hemlocks, feels primeval, with the scent of pine and the sound of the river creating an atmosphere of tranquility and solitude.

## Hiking Trails

Olympic National Park's hiking trails offer some of the most varied and rewarding experiences in the Pacific Northwest, from easy walks through lush rainforests to strenuous climbs to alpine ridges.

### *Hoh River Trail to Five Mile Island*

Length: 10 miles (16 km) round-trip
Elevation Change: Minimal
Difficulty: Easy to Moderate

The Hoh River Trail offers a stunning journey through the heart of the Hoh Rainforest, following the river as it winds through dense stands of Sitka spruce, hemlock, and ferns. The trail is relatively flat, making it accessible to most hikers, but the real magic lies in the lush, green surroundings. As you walk, the moss-draped trees seem to glow in the filtered light, and the air is filled with the earthy scent of the forest. Five Mile Island, a picturesque spot along the river with views of the surrounding peaks, is a perfect turnaround point for a day hike.

### *Hurricane Hill Trail*

Length: 3.4 miles (5.5 km) round-trip
Elevation Change: 700 feet (213 meters)
Difficulty: Moderate

This popular trail offers some of the best views in the park, with a relatively gentle climb to a summit that provides panoramic vistas of the Olympic Mountains, the Strait of Juan de Fuca, and, on clear days, Vancouver Island. The trail is paved in sections, making it accessible for families and those looking for a shorter hike with a big payoff. As you ascend, the meadows are filled with wildflowers, and marmots can often be seen sunning themselves on the rocks. The summit provides a 360-degree view that is nothing short of breathtaking, showcasing the full range of the park's diverse landscapes.

### *Sol Duc Falls Trail*

Length: 1.6 miles (2.6 km) round-trip
Elevation Change: 200 feet (61 meters)
Difficulty: Easy

This short but stunning hike leads to one of the park's most beautiful waterfalls, where the Sol Duc River splits into multiple channels and cascades over a rocky ledge into a mossy canyon. The trail begins at the Sol Duc Hot Springs Resort and meanders through a lush old-growth forest filled with towering trees and ferns. The sound of the falls grows louder as you approach, and the sight of the water crashing into the canyon below is mesmerizing. This easy trail is perfect for families and offers a quick escape into the beauty of the Olympic rainforest.

### *Cape Alava Trail (Ozette Triangle)*

Length: 9.4 miles (15.1 km) loop
Elevation Change: Minimal
Difficulty: Moderate

For those seeking a coastal adventure, the Cape Alava Trail offers a unique hike that combines forest, coastal, and cultural experiences. The trail begins near Lake Ozette and follows a series of boardwalks through dense coastal forest before emerging onto a wild, rocky shoreline. Cape Alava is the westernmost point in the contiguous United States, and the beach is dotted with tide pools, sea stacks, and ancient petroglyphs carved by the Makah people. The loop continues along the coast to Sand Point before returning through the forest, offering a complete and immersive experience of Olympic's diverse ecosystems.

## Other Activities: Beyond the Trails – Experiencing Olympic's Wild Beauty

Beyond hiking, Olympic National Park offers many activities that showcase its stunning landscapes and rich biodiversity.

### *Kayaking and Canoeing*

The park's rivers and lakes are perfect for kayaking and canoeing, providing a unique perspective on its breathtaking scenery. Popular spots like Lake Crescent and the Quinault River invite paddlers to explore their pristine waters. As you glide along the surface, you'll be surrounded by towering mountains and lush forests that seem to rise straight from the water.

Paddling on Lake Crescent, known for its striking blue color, offers a serene experience where you can enjoy the tranquility and beauty of the environment. Keep your eyes peeled for wildlife along the shores—otters may be spotted playing in the water while bald eagles soar overhead, scanning for fish. For a thrilling experience, consider joining a guided kayaking tour, where you can learn about the area's ecology and history while navigating the waters.

### Tidepooling on the Coast

For those interested in the park's marine life, tidepooling along the coast reveals a hidden world of colorful sea creatures. The rocky shores of places like Rialto Beach and Second Beach offer excellent opportunities to explore the diverse intertidal ecosystems. As the tide recedes, you'll encounter vibrant anemones, starfish, and crabs scuttling among the rocks. Joining a ranger-led tidepooling program can enhance this experience, as rangers share insights about the delicate balance of these habitats and the fascinating creatures that inhabit them. Learning about the adaptations of these species and their role in the ecosystem adds depth to your exploration, making it a visual feast and an educational adventure.

### Surfing and Beachcombing

The park's beaches, with their stunning backdrops of rugged cliffs and ancient forests, are also great spots for surfing and beach-combing. Whether you're a seasoned surfer or a beginner looking to catch your first wave, the waves at La Push offer exhilarating conditions. For those who prefer a more leisurely activity, beach-combing provides a chance to search for unique treasures washed ashore. Agates, driftwood, and seashells can be found scattered along the sand, each telling a story of the ocean's journey. Take your time wandering along the shoreline, allowing the sounds of crashing waves and the scent of salt air to invigorate your senses.

### Wildlife Watching

Wildlife watching is another highlight of Olympic National Park, where the diverse habitats support a rich array of species. From the misty rainforests to alpine meadows and coastal bluffs, the park is home to elk, black bears, mountain goats, and an impressive variety of bird species. Early mornings and late afternoons are the best times to spot wildlife as they are most active during these cooler hours. Consider joining a ranger-led wildlife program to learn more about the park's inhabitants, their behaviors, and the ongoing conservation efforts to protect these incredible species. Observing these majestic creatures in their natural habitat adds an extra layer of excitement to your visit.

*Fishing*

For those seeking a tranquil day on the water, fishing in Olympic's pristine rivers and lakes can be a relaxing way to connect with nature. The park has several fishing spots, including the Hoh River and Lake Ozette, where anglers can cast their lines for native species such as cutthroat trout and salmon. Be sure to check fishing regulations and obtain any necessary permits before you start. As you fish, enjoy the peaceful surroundings, with the sound of water flowing and birds singing overhead, creating a perfect backdrop for a day of relaxation.

*Cultural and Educational Programs*

Participating in cultural and educational programs can deepen your understanding of Olympic National Park's history and ecology. Ranger-led talks, workshops, and demonstrations offer insights into the region's Indigenous cultures, the park's unique ecosystems, and ongoing conservation efforts. Engaging with these programs enhances your experience and fosters a greater appreciation for the importance of preserving these remarkable landscapes for future generations.

## Flora and Fauna: The Park's Diverse Ecosystems

Olympic National Park is home to some of the most diverse ecosystems in North America, ranging from temperate rainforests and alpine meadows to coastal tide pools and river valleys. The park's rainforests, among the wettest places in the continental United States, are filled with towering Sitka spruce, western hemlock, and Douglas fir, draped in moss and lichen. The forest floor is carpeted with ferns, salal, and huckleberry, creating a lush, green tapestry that feels almost otherworldly.

The park's mountains support alpine and subalpine ecosystems, where wildflowers bloom in vibrant displays during the brief summer months. Lupines, avalanche lilies, and paintbrush thrive in the meadows, attracting pollinators such as butterflies and hummingbirds. In the higher elevations, hardy species like mountain goats and marmots have adapted to the harsh conditions, finding shelter among the rocks and ridges.

Olympic's coastal areas are equally rich in biodiversity, with rocky shores, sandy beaches, and tide pools that support a variety of marine life. Sea stars, anemones, and crabs are common in the intertidal zones, while seals, sea lions, and even gray whales can be spotted offshore. The park's rivers and lakes are home to salmon, steelhead, and other native fish species, highlighting the interconnectedness of the park's diverse habitats.

## Best Campgrounds and Accommodation Options

Camping in Olympic National Park offers a chance to fully immerse yourself in the park's diverse environments. The Hoh Campground, located in the heart of the Hoh Rainforest, is a favorite for its proximity to the park's lushest trails and the soothing sound of the river nearby. Sites are nestled among towering trees, providing shade and a sense of seclusion.

Kalaloch (KLAY-lock) Campground, set along the park's wild coastline, offers stunning ocean views and easy access to the beach. Falling asleep to the sound of crashing waves and waking up to misty coastal mornings is an experience unique to the Olympic's coastal environment. The campground also offers ranger-led programs and tidepooling opportunities, making it a great spot for families.

Backcountry camping is available for those looking to explore the park's more remote areas, with permits required for overnight stays. Popular backcountry sites include those along the Enchanted Valley and Hoh River trails, offering solitude and the chance to camp in some of the park's most beautiful and secluded locations.

## Mysterious Sightings and Encounters in Olympic National Park

### *The Howling of the Hoh Rainforest*

In the late 1990s, a group of experienced hikers set out to explore the dense, mystical beauty of the Hoh Rainforest, known for its towering trees and lush vegetation. As they ventured deeper into the woods, the tranquility of the rainforest was suddenly shattered by an unearthly howling sound that echoed through the trees. The noise was unlike anything they had ever encountered—a mix of deep growls and eerie wails reverberating in a way that sent shivers down their spines.

The hikers stopped in their tracks, exchanging nervous glances as the howling continued, seeming to surround them from all sides. It was an unsettling experience, and despite their curiosity, they felt an instinctual urge to leave the area. The sound grew fainter as they retreated, but they couldn't shake the feeling that they were not alone.

Upon returning to civilization, the hikers reported their experience to park rangers, who informed them they were not the first to hear such mysterious sounds in the Hoh Rainforest. Rangers noted that while various animals could produce strange noises, none were ever identified as the source of the howling that had unnerved visitors over the years. The incident became part of the local lore, adding to the allure of the Hoh Rainforest as a place where the natural world can still evoke wonder—and perhaps a little fear.

### The Vanishing Woman of Ruby Beach

Visitors to Ruby Beach have recounted stories of a woman dressed in white who appears near the shore during foggy evenings. Witnesses claim she walks along the beach, often looking out to sea. When approached, she vanishes into thin air, leaving no trace behind. This has led to speculation about her identity and connection to local folklore.

### Bigfoot Sightings

Olympic National Park has a rich history of Bigfoot sightings, with numerous reports from visitors claiming encounters with the elusive creature. One notable incident occurred in 1993 when a group of campers in the Quinault area claimed to see a large, hairy figure moving through the trees. They described hearing strange vocalizations and felt an overwhelming sense of dread. They reported the sighting to park rangers, who noted it as one of many similar encounters in the area.

## Practical Travel Tips and Planning Information

Olympic National Park is best visited in late spring through early fall when the weather is mild and the park's trails are fully accessible. Be prepared for rapidly changing conditions, especially in the mountains, where snow can linger into summer and rain is always possible. Pack layers, sturdy hiking boots, and plenty of water, as many of the park's trails are long and remote.

The park is vast and diverse, so plan your route in advance to make the most of your visit. The Olympic Peninsula Loop Drive offers a scenic journey through the park's varied landscapes, with numerous pullouts and trailheads along the way. Be sure to check tide charts before visiting coastal areas, as some trails and beaches are only accessible at low tide.

Safety is paramount in Olympic's wilderness. Stay on marked trails, keep a safe distance from wildlife, and always carry a map and compass when hiking in remote areas. If you plan to explore the backcountry, be prepared for rugged terrain and practice Leave No Trace principles to protect the park's pristine environment.

## Conclusion: Inspiring Further Exploration

Olympic National Park is a place of unparalleled beauty and diversity, where rainforests, mountains, and coastlines converge to create a landscape unlike any other. As you explore its lush valleys, climb its rugged peaks, and walk its wild shores, let yourself be inspired by the park's raw, untamed spirit. This is a place where nature reigns supreme, where every trail, beach, and ridge offer a new adventure and a deeper connection to the natural world.

Whether you're soaking in a hot spring, watching elk graze in a misty meadow, or gazing out at the endless expanse of the Pacific Ocean, Olympic National Park invites you to discover its secrets and embrace its wild beauty. Let the park's diverse landscapes remind you of the power and resilience of nature and the importance of protecting these special places for future generations. Explore, protect, and cherish the Olympic Peninsula's wild heart. Let its timeless beauty stay with you long after you've gone.

# SEVEN

# Crater Lake National Park

## THE DEEP BLUE WONDER OF THE CASCADES

 *"The deep blue of Crater Lake is one of the most beautiful sights in the world."*

John C. Van Dyke

### Introduction: The Park's History and Significance

C rater Lake National Park, nestled in the southern Cascades of Oregon, is home to the deepest lake in the United States and one of the most visually striking landscapes in the world. With its sapphire-blue waters, sheer cliffs, and the hauntingly beautiful Wizard Island, Crater Lake is a natural wonder born from a cataclysmic volcanic eruption over 7,700 years ago. The park's history is as deep and layered as the lake itself, shaped by ancient volcanic forces, the traditions of Native American tribes, and the tireless efforts of conservationists who recognized the importance of preserving this unique environment.

The story of Crater Lake begins with the eruption of Mount Mazama (muh-ZAH-muh), a once-towering volcano that stood at nearly 12,000 feet. In a cataclysmic event, the mountain erupted in a massive explosion that sent ash and pumice raining down for hundreds of miles, collapsing the summit into a giant caldera. Over centuries, rain and snowmelt filled the caldera, creating the lake we see today—a brilliant, crystal-clear body of water with a depth of nearly 1,943 feet. For the Klamath tribes, who have lived in the region for thousands of years, Crater Lake was a place of deep spiritual significance. Legends tell of a great battle between the spirit of the sky and the spirit of the underworld, which resulted in the mountain's destruction and the creation of the lake. To the Klamath people, the lake was sacred, a place of power and mystery, and they would not approach its shores out of respect and awe.

European American exploration of the lake began in the mid-19th century when prospectors searching for gold stumbled upon the awe-inspiring sight of the lake's deep blue waters. In 1853, John Wesley Hillman, a young prospector, became the first known European American to gaze upon the lake, which he called "Deep Blue Lake" due to its startling color. Over the next several decades, word of the lake spread, drawing adventurers, artists, and scientists who sought to understand its origins and capture its beauty.

One of the most significant figures in the lake's history was William Gladstone Steel, often called the "Father of Crater Lake." Steel first heard about the lake as a boy and became captivated by its mystery. In the late 1800s, he dedicated himself to the lake's preservation, tirelessly lobbying for its protection as a national park. Steel's efforts paid off in 1902 when President Theodore Roosevelt established Crater Lake National Park, making it the fifth national park in the United States and the only one created solely to protect a lake.

Today, Crater Lake is recognized not only for its stunning beauty but also for its ecological and geological significance. The lake's pristine waters, fed entirely by rain and snow, are among the clearest in the world, and the surrounding caldera walls and volcanic formations provide a living laboratory for scientists studying volcanic activity, climate change, and ecosystem resilience. Conservation efforts focus on preserving the lake's clarity, protecting native species, and managing the impacts of climate change, which threatens the park's delicate balance of snowpack, water levels, and biodiversity.

Crater Lake's cultural significance continues to inspire visitors from around the world. Whether standing on the rim and gazing into the impossibly blue depths, hiking through ancient forests, or simply absorbing the quiet majesty of this volcanic wonder, the park offers a profound connection to the natural world and a reminder of the powerful forces that shape our planet.

## Fascinating Facts About Crater Lake National Park

1. **Deepest Lake**: Crater Lake is the deepest lake in the United States, reaching a depth of 1,943 feet (592 meters).
2. **Volcanic Origin**: The lake was formed about 7,700 years ago after a major volcanic eruption caused Mount Mazama to collapse.
3. **No Rivers Feed It**: Crater Lake has no inlet or outlet rivers; its water level is maintained solely by precipitation, including rain and snow.
4. **Stunning Blue Color**: The lake's striking blue color is due to its purity and depth, allowing it to absorb all light spectrum colors except blue.

1. **Wizard Island**: The iconic Wizard Island is a volcanic cinder cone that rises 763 feet above the lake's surface and is accessible by boat tours.
2. **National Park Status**: Crater Lake was designated as a national park on May 22, 1902, making it the fifth national park in the United States.
3. **Snowfall Record**: The park receives an average of 533 inches (1,356 cm) of snow annually, making it one of the snowiest places in the country.
4. **Unique Ecosystem**: Crater Lake is home to several endemic species, including the Crater Lake sculpin, a fish found nowhere else.
5. **Cave Exploration**: Crater Lake has numerous lava tubes, the most popular of which is the Vidae Falls Cave, where visitors can explore unique geological formations.
6. **Historic Lodge**: The Crater Lake Lodge, built in 1915, offers stunning views of the lake and is listed on the National Register of Historic Places.

## Key Highlights and Must-See Landmarks

Crater Lake National Park is a feast for the senses, where every turn reveals new perspectives of the lake's brilliant blue waters, volcanic formations, and surrounding forests. The park's center-piece is Crater Lake itself, a vast expanse of water that shimmers in shades of blue, ranging from deep indigo to vibrant turquoise. The lake's color results from its incredible depth and clarity, allowing it to absorb all light colors except blue. Gazing into the lake, it's easy to feel a sense of awe and wonder, as if looking into the Earth's soul.

One of the most iconic features of Crater Lake is Wizard Island, a cinder cone that rises 763 feet above the lake's surface, crowned with a small crater at its summit. Named for resembling a sorcerer's hat, Wizard Island is a popular destination for visitors who want to explore the lake up close. Boat tours offer the unique opportunity to circle the island, disembark, and hike to the top, where panoramic views of the lake and surrounding caldera walls await. The rugged, volcanic landscape of the island feels otherworldly, with twisted lava flows and stunted trees adding to the sense of stepping back in time.

The Rim Drive, a 33-mile loop that circles the caldera, offers some of the best views of Crater Lake and its surrounding landscapes. The road winds along the rim, with numerous pullouts and viewpoints that provide breathtaking perspectives of the lake from different angles. Watchman Overlook is one of the most stunning overlooks, where a short hike leads to the historic Watchman Fire Lookout, perched high above the lake. From here, the sweeping view of Wizard Island, the deep blue waters, and the distant peaks of the Cascades is unforgettable, especially at sunrise or sunset when the colors are at their most vibrant.

Another must-see landmark is Phantom Ship, a jagged rock formation that resembles a ghostly ship sailing across the lake's waters. Rising from the southeast corner of the lake, Phantom Ship is composed of volcanic rock that predates the eruption of Mount Mazama, making it one of the oldest features in the park. The formation's spires and cliffs create an eerie silhouette against the lake's surface, especially when shrouded in mist or illuminated by the soft light of dawn.

For those interested in the park's geology, the Cleetwood Cove Trail offers a rare opportunity to descend from the rim to the lake's edge. This steep, 2.2-mile round-trip hike leads down the caldera wall, offering up-close views of the lake's striking blue water and the chance to dip your toes in its chilly depths.

Cleetwood Cove is the only legal access to the lake's shoreline. It is a popular spot for swimming, fishing, and embarking on boat tours to Wizard Island.

## Hidden Gems: Lesser-Known Spots Worth Exploring

While the main attractions draw the crowds, Crater Lake National Park also offers hidden gems that provide a quieter, more intimate experience of the park's beauty. One such spot is the Pinnacles, a striking collection of volcanic spires located in the park's southeast corner. Formed by volcanic gases escaping through ash deposits during the eruption of Mount Mazama, the Pinnacles are tall, needle-like formations that rise dramatically from the valley floor. The Pinnacles Overlook provides a close-up view of these other-worldly spires, which are best seen in the soft light of morning or late afternoon when the shadows create a stunning contrast.

Another hidden treasure is Plaikni (PLAKE-nee) Falls, a serene waterfall off Pinnacles Road. The 2-mile round-trip trail to the falls winds through a lush forest of wildflowers, mountain hemlocks, and whitebark pines, offering a gentle, shaded walk that ends at the base of a picturesque cascade. The falls spill gracefully over moss-covered rocks into a quiet pool, creating a peaceful oasis that feels far removed from the more bustling areas of the park. Plaikni Falls is a perfect spot for a picnic or a quiet moment of reflection, surrounded by the sights and sounds of nature.

For those looking to escape the rim's more popular viewpoints, the Garfield Peak Trail offers a challenging but rewarding hike to one of the highest points accessible in the park. The trail climbs steeply from Crater Lake Lodge, ascending through rocky switchbacks and alpine meadows to a summit with breathtaking views of the entire lake, Wizard Island, and the surrounding Cascades. The hike is strenuous, but the panoramic vistas from the top are well worth the effort, providing a perspective on the park that few visitors get to see.

## Hiking Trails

Crater Lake's hiking trails offer diverse experiences, from easy strolls along the rim to more strenuous climbs that provide sweeping views of the lake and surrounding landscape.

### *Cleetwood Cove Trail*

Length: 2.2 miles (3.5 km) round-trip
Elevation Change: 700 feet (213 meters)
Difficulty: Strenuous

The Cleetwood Cove Trail is the only trail that allows visitors to descend to the lake's edge, providing a rare opportunity to experience Crater Lake up close. The trail is steep and challenging, descending 700 feet in just over a mile, but the reward is worth it. At the lake's edge, you can swim in the crystal-clear water, fish for native kokanee salmon and rainbow trout, or relax and enjoy the stunning views. For the adventurous, boat tours depart from Cleetwood Cove, offering the chance to explore Wizard Island and the lake's unique volcanic features.

### *Garfield Peak Trail*

Length: 3.6 miles (5.8 km) round-trip
Elevation Change: 1,000 feet (305 meters)
Difficulty: Moderate to Strenuous

One of the most rewarding hikes in the park, the Garfield Peak Trail, offers panoramic views of Crater Lake, Wizard Island, and the surrounding Cascades. The trail begins near Crater Lake Lodge and climbs steadily through alpine meadows filled with wildflowers. As you ascend, the views become more expansive, with each switchback revealing a new angle on the lake's deep blue waters. The final push to the summit is steep, but the 360-degree view from the top is unparalleled, providing a bird's-eye perspective of the entire park.

### Watchman Peak Trail

Length: 1.6 miles (2.6 km) round-trip
Elevation Change: 420 feet (128 meters)
Difficulty: Moderate

This short but scenic trail leads to the historic Watchman Fire Lookout, perched high above Crater Lake's rim. The trail begins at Watchman Overlook and climbs gradually to the lookout, offering stunning views of Wizard Island and the lake's caldera. The lookout, built in 1932, provides a glimpse into the park's fire management history and offers one of the best vantage points for watching the sunset over the lake. The colors of the water shift from deep blue to fiery orange and purple as the sun dips below the horizon, creating a truly magical experience.

### Plaikni Falls Trail

Length: 2 miles (3.2 km) round-trip
Elevation Change: 100 feet (30 meters)
Difficulty: Easy

The Plaikni Falls Trail offers a gentle, family-friendly hike to one of the park's hidden waterfalls. The trail meanders through a lush forest of mountain hemlocks and wildflowers, with interpretive signs along the way that highlight the park's unique flora and geol-ogy. The trail's gradual incline makes it accessible to hikers of all ages, and the reward at the end—a peaceful waterfall cascading over moss-covered rocks—creates a perfect spot to relax and enjoy the tranquility of Crater Lake's lesser-known landscapes.

## Other Activities: Beyond the Trails – Exploring Crater Lake's Deep Blue Mysteries

Beyond hiking, Crater Lake offers a variety of activities that show-case its unique volcanic and aquatic environments, allowing visi-tors to experience the park's beauty in diverse and exciting ways.

### *Boat Tours on Crater Lake*

One of the most popular ways to experience Crater Lake is through boat tours, which provide an unforgettable perspective of the caldera's stunning scenery. Guided trips navigate the clear, deep blue waters, with knowledgeable guides sharing fascinating insights into the lake's geology, ecology, and rich history. During the tour, visitors can stop at Wizard Island, a volcanic island that rises dramatically from the lake's surface. Here, you can explore the island's hiking trails, enjoy a picnic, and soak in panoramic views of the caldera. Another highlight is Phantom Ship, a rocky outcrop that resembles a ghostly ship sailing through the water, providing a perfect backdrop for photos. The boat tours offer close-up views of these iconic features and the chance to learn about the ongoing conservation efforts to preserve this unique environment.

## *Fishing in Crater Lake*

For those interested in fishing, Crater Lake's pristine waters are home to non-native kokanee salmon and rainbow trout, introduced in the late 1800s. Fishing is allowed without a license, making it accessible for both casual anglers and those looking to cast their lines in a truly spectacular setting. Popular spots for fishing include the shores of Cleetwood Cove, which serves as the only access point to the lake for anglers, and Wizard Island, where you can fish while enjoying the serene beauty of the surroundings. The lake's clear waters provide a unique fishing experience, with the added thrill of being surrounded by one of the world's most stunning landscapes. Whether reeling in a catch or simply enjoying the tranquility, fishing at Crater Lake is an adventure unlike any other.

## *Winter Wonderland Activities*

In winter, Crater Lake transforms into a snowy wonderland, offering a plethora of activities for winter sports enthusiasts. The park's deep snowpack and dramatic winter scenery create a picturesque setting for snowshoeing, cross-country skiing, and snowmobiling. Numerous marked trails provide access to the rim, leading you through enchanting forests and open snow-filled meadows. For those seeking a guided experience, ranger-led snowshoe walks offer a fun and educational way to explore the park's winter environment. As you trek through the serene landscape, rangers share insights into the lake's natural history, the adaptations of its plants and animals, and the cultural significance of this remarkable place.

## *Stargazing*

Crater Lake's high elevation and remote location make it an ideal spot for stargazing. Away from city lights, the park offers stunning night sky views, allowing visitors to witness the brilliance of the Milky Way and countless constellations. Popular stargazing locations include the rim of the caldera and designated viewpoints. The park often hosts ranger-led stargazing programs, where visitors can learn about celestial navigation, constellations, and the science behind the universe's wonders. Bringing a telescope or simply lying back on a blanket to enjoy the star-filled sky can be a wonderful experience.

## *Photography*

Photography at Crater Lake is an adventure in itself, with countless opportunities to capture the breathtaking landscapes and vibrant colors of the lake. The unique blue hue of the water, especially on sunny days, provides a stunning contrast to the dark volcanic rock surrounding the caldera. Sunrise and sunset are particularly perfect times for photographers, as the light bathes the lake and its surroundings in warm tones. Popular spots for photography include the rim viewpoints, where you can frame your shots with the lake as a backdrop, and the rugged cliffs of Wizard Island. Each season brings its own beauty, allowing photographers to capture the park's changing moods and landscapes.

## *Camping Under the Stars*

Camping at Crater Lake allows you to immerse yourself in the park's natural beauty and enjoy the serene atmosphere of the wilderness. The park features campgrounds that offer access to hiking trails, fishing spots, and stunning viewpoints. Imagine setting up your tent surrounded by towering trees, with the sounds of nature as your soundtrack. As night falls, the clear skies provide excellent stargazing opportunities, allowing you to see constellations and celestial events with breathtaking clarity. Sharing stories around a campfire while gazing up at the stars is a quintessential experience for many visitors.

### *Cultural and Educational Programs*

Engaging in cultural and educational programs at Crater Lake enhances your understanding of the park's history and ecology. Ranger-led talks and workshops cover a wide range of topics, from the geology of the caldera to the importance of conservation efforts. Participating in these programs provides a deeper appreciation for the natural wonders surrounding you. It fosters a greater commitment to preserving this incredible landscape for future generations.

## Flora and Fauna: The Park's Diverse Ecosystems

Crater Lake National Park is home to various ecosystems that support a diverse array of plant and animal life, from subalpine forests to alpine meadows and volcanic landscapes. The park's forests are dominated by mountain hemlock, lodgepole pine, and whitebark pine, with stands of ancient trees that have withstood the harsh volcanic environment for centuries. In summer, the meadows around the lake burst into bloom with wildflowers, including lupines, paintbrush, and monkeyflowers, creating a vibrant contrast against the stark volcanic rock.

The park's clear waters support a limited but unique aquatic ecosystem, with native invertebrates and introduced fish species coexisting in the lake's deep, cold environment. The absence of streams feeding into the lake means that the water is exceptionally pure, supporting a delicate balance of life that is sensitive to environmental changes.

Wildlife is abundant in the park, with black bears, mule deer, and mountain lions among the larger mammals that roam the forests. Smaller creatures, like chipmunks, squirrels, and pikas, can often be seen scurrying among the rocks and meadows. Birdwatchers can spot various species, from Clark's nutcrackers and Steller's jays to bald eagles and peregrine falcons soaring above the lake's rim.

## Best Campgrounds and Accommodation Options

Camping in Crater Lake National Park offers a chance to fully immerse yourself in the park's stunning landscapes. Mazama Campground, located just seven miles south of the lake, is the park's main camping area. It offers tent and RV sites nestled among old-growth forests. The campground provides easy access to the rim and amenities like restrooms, showers, and a camp store, making it a convenient base for exploring the park.

For those seeking a more rustic experience, Lost Creek Campground offers a quieter alternative with just 16 tent sites. It provides a more intimate connection to the park's wilderness. The campground's proximity to some of the park's less-traveled trails makes it an excellent choice for hikers exploring the hidden corners of Crater Lake.

The historic Crater Lake Lodge, perched on the rim with breathtaking lake views, offers a more comfortable stay for those who prefer indoor accommodations. Built in 1915, the lodge combines rustic charm with modern amenities, providing a cozy retreat with stunning views of the lake and surrounding caldera. Guests can relax by the fireplace, enjoy a meal in the dining room, and watch the sunset over the lake from the lodge's expansive terrace.

## Mysterious Sightings at Crater Lake National Park

### *Ghost Campfires of Crater Lake*

Visitors to Crater Lake National Park have long shared accounts of eerie encounters with ghostly campfires flickering in the night. One particularly compelling story comes from a group of campers who set up their site near the park's rim one summer evening. As twilight descended, they gathered around their own fire, roasting marshmallows and sharing ghost stories, the crackling flames casting long shadows on the surrounding trees.

They noticed a distant light flickering among the trees as the night deepened. Initially dismissing it as another group of campers, they continued their festivities. However, the light grew brighter and closer, illuminating the area with an ethereal glow. Curious, they decided to investigate, leaving their campsite and trekking toward the mysterious light.

When they arrived, the group found nothing—no campers, no tents, just a faint glow that seemed to dance among the trees. The air was still, and an uneasy silence enveloped them. It was as if the light was aware of their presence, flickering in response to their movements. Just as they were about to turn back, the light vanished, leaving them in complete darkness.

Feeling a mix of thrill and unease, they hurried back to their campsite. The experience left them with an unsettling feeling, but they brushed it off as a trick of the light or their imagination. However, later that night, they heard soft laughter and the faint sounds of a campfire—crackling, popping, and even the low murmur of conversation drifting through the trees. They exchanged nervous glances, wondering if they had accidentally stumbled upon a ghostly gathering of park visitors from another time.

Though they never saw anyone, the campers agreed that the experience was unlike any they had encountered before. The whispers of laughter continued throughout the night, keeping them both intrigued and on edge, as if the park spirits were inviting them into a secret world just beyond their sight. The following morning, they recounted their experience to other visitors at the lodge, only to learn that many had reported similar sightings of ghostly campfires over the years.

### *The Haunted Crater Lake Lodge*

Crater Lake Lodge, built in 1915, has a reputation for being haunted. Staff and guests alike have reported strange occurrences over the years, including doors opening and closing on their own, mysterious footsteps in empty hallways, and lights flickering without explanation. One staff member shared a story of hearing a piano playing softly late at night in the common area. When they investigated, they found no one there, but the piano continued to play for a few moments before falling silent. The lodge's long history and the many visitors it has hosted add to the haunting lore, leaving many wondering if past guests' spirits linger within its walls.

### *The "Nessie" Monster Sighting*

In 2008, a visitor claimed to have spotted a creature resembling the legendary Loch Ness Monster while kayaking on Crater Lake. The visitor reported seeing a large, dark shape moving beneath the water's surface, creating ripples that disturbed the otherwise calm lake. Describing the creature as long and serpentine, the witness noted that it surfaced briefly before disappearing into the depths. Although the sighting remains unconfirmed, it sparked intrigue and conversation among other park visitors, adding to the park's mystique.

## Practical Travel Tips and Planning Information

Crater Lake is best visited from late spring through early fall when the park's roads and trails are fully accessible. Snow can linger on the rim well into June, and the park's high elevation means that weather conditions can change rapidly. Pack layers, sunscreen, and plenty of water, as the sun's reflection off the lake can intensify UV exposure, and the park's dry air can quickly lead to dehydration.

The Rim Drive is a must-do for any visit, but it's best to start early in the day to avoid crowds and enjoy the changing lights on the lake. The drive offers numerous pullouts and overlooks, each providing a different perspective of the lake and its surrounding landscapes. Be sure to check for road closures, as some sections of the drive may be closed due to snow or maintenance.

Always stay on designated trails when hiking, as the steep caldera walls are unstable and dangerous. The lake's waters are incredibly pure, so be mindful of your impact and follow Leave No Trace principles to help preserve this delicate environment. If you plan to fish, be aware that only artificial lures are allowed, and all fish must be caught and released.

## Conclusion: Inspiring Further Exploration

Crater Lake National Park is a place of profound beauty and geological wonder. The deep blue waters of an ancient caldera invite you to explore, reflect, and connect with the natural world. Whether hiking along the rim, gazing into the lake's depths from a quiet overlook, or standing on the shores of Wizard Island, the park offers moments of awe that stay with you long after you've left.

This landscape is shaped by fire and ice, by violent and beautiful forces, and it stands as a reminder of the Earth's power to create and transform. Let the majesty of Crater Lake inspire you to explore further, protect the wild places that remain, and cherish the natural wonders that make our world so extraordinary. As you leave the park, take with you a sense of the lake's timeless beauty and the enduring spirit of the land, and let it inspire you to seek out the wonders that await beyond every horizon.

# EIGHT

# Haleakalā National Park

## THE HOUSE OF THE SUN

*"There's nothing quite like standing on the summit of Haleakalā, watching the sunrise—it's as if the world is reborn."*

Unknown

### Introduction: The Park's History and Significance

Haleakalā (hah-leh-AH-kah-lah) National Park, rising majestically from the tropical landscape of Maui, is a place of stark contrasts and breathtaking beauty. Known as the "House of the Sun," this massive shield volcano dominates the island's southeastern side, its summit reaching an impressive 10,023 feet above sea level. The park encompasses over 30,000 acres of diverse landscapes, from the arid, otherworldly summit to lush rainforests filled with vibrant, endemic species found nowhere else on Earth. For centuries, Haleakalā has captivated the hearts and minds of those who encounter it, from the Native Hawaiians who revered it as a sacred place to the explorers and conservationists who recognized its unique ecological and cultural significance.

The name Haleakalā translates to "House of the Sun," a title rooted in Hawaiian mythology. According to legend, the demigod Māui stood on the volcano's summit and lassoed the sun, slowing its journey across the sky to lengthen the day and bring more light to the world. For Native Hawaiians, the summit of Haleakalā was more than just a dramatic vantage point—it was a place of profound spiritual importance where the land, the sky, and the heavens intersected. The crater was considered a sacred site, a place where kahuna (priests) performed ceremonies and rituals to honor the gods and seek guidance for their people.

The arrival of European explorers in the late 18th century marked the beginning of significant changes to Haleakalā's landscape. In the 19th century, cattle ranching and introduced species such as goats and pigs began to take a toll on the native vegetation, leading to erosion and the decline of fragile ecosystems. The unique flora and fauna of the mountain, which had evolved in isolation over millions of years, faced unprecedented threats from habitat destruction and invasive species.

Recognizing the need to protect this extraordinary landscape, efforts to establish Haleakalā as a national park began in the early 20th century. In 1916, Haleakalā became part of Hawaii National Park, along with Kīlauea (key-lah-way-ah) and Mauna Loa (Maunah Loh-ah) on the Big Island. It wasn't until 1961 that Haleakalā was designated as its own national park, highlighting its distinct ecosystems and cultural heritage. Today, Haleakalā National Park is a sanctuary for rare and endangered species, including the nēnē (Hawaiian goose) and the silversword plant, which blooms only once in its lifetime before dying. The park is also a place of continued cultural significance for Native Hawaiians, who maintain a deep connection to the land and its sacred sites.

Conservation efforts within the park are focused on protecting and restoring native habitats, controlling invasive species, and preserving the cultural heritage of the Hawaiian people. The summit of Haleakalā is not just a geological wonder but a living link to Hawaii's past, present, and future—a place where the stories of the land and its people are written in the volcanic rock and the rare, resilient plants that cling to life in the harsh, windswept environment.

## Fascinating Facts About Haleakalā National Park

1. **Massive Crater**: Haleakalā's summit crater is 7 miles long, 2.5 miles wide, and over 2,600 feet deep, making it one of the largest craters in the world.
2. **Biodiversity Hotspot**: The park is home to over 1,500 species of native plants and animals, many of which are found nowhere else on Earth.
3. **Endangered Species**: Haleakalā is a sanctuary for several endangered species, including the Hawaiian goose (nene) and the silversword plant.
4. **Cultural Significance**: The park is sacred to Native Hawaiians, who believe Haleakalā is the home of the demigod Maui, who lassoed the sun.
5. **Weather Extremes**: Even in summer, the summit can experience extreme weather conditions, including temperatures below freezing.
6. **Unique Ecosystems**: The park contains a variety of ecosystems, from lush rainforests at lower elevations to arid desert conditions at the summit.

7. **Volcanic History**: Haleakalā is a dormant volcano whose last eruption occurred in the 18th century, around 1790.
8. **Sunrise and Sunset**: Watching the sunrise from the summit is popular, with many visitors rising early to witness the breathtaking views.
9. **Elevation Variation**: The park's elevation ranges from sea level to 10,023 feet at the summit, resulting in diverse climate conditions and habitats.
10. **Rare Plants**: The park is home to the endangered Haleakalā silversword, a striking plant that can take up to 50 years to flower.

## Key Highlights and Must-See Landmarks

Haleakalā National Park is a land of dramatic landscapes and stunning vistas, where every corner of the park offers a new perspective on the island's diverse natural beauty. The most iconic feature of the park is the massive Haleakalā Crater, a vast, open expanse that stretches nearly 7 miles across and 2,600 feet deep. Despite its name, the crater is not the result of a single volcanic explosion but rather a series of erosional valleys carved by wind and water over millennia. The landscape within the crater is stark and surreal, with cinder cones, lava flows, and red, black, and orange sands resembling Mars's surface.

One of the best ways to experience the crater's vastness is from the summit at Puʻu ʻUlaʻula (POO-oo OO-lah OO-lah) or just (Red Hill), the highest point in the park. Here, at 10,023 feet above sea level, visitors are treated to panoramic views that stretch across the island and out to the Pacific Ocean. On a clear day, you can see as far as the Big Island of Hawaii. If you're lucky, you might witness the phenomenon known as the "Brocken specter," a circular rainbow that appears around your shadow cast on the clouds below.

Sunrise at Haleakalā is one of the park's most famous and unforgettable experiences. Hundreds of visitors gather at the summit in the pre-dawn darkness each morning, braving the cold and wind to witness the first light of daybreak over the volcanic landscape. As the sun rises, it bathes the crater in a golden glow, illuminating the cinder cones and casting long shadows across the rugged terrain. The sight is nothing short of magical, and it's easy to see why ancient Hawaiians believed this place to be the dwelling of the gods.

The Sliding Sands Trail offers a challenging but rewarding hike into the heart of the crater. The trail descends steeply from the summit, winding through a landscape of vibrant cinders, lava fields, and rare silversword plants that seem to glow in the morning light. The trail's descent into the crater provides an intimate look at the park's volcanic features, with each step taking you deeper into a world shaped by fire and time. While the hike down is relatively easy, the climb back up is strenuous, and the high elevation can make the return journey a test of endurance.

For those seeking a different perspective, the Kīpahulu (kee-pah-HOO-loo) District on the park's southeastern coast offers a lush, tropical contrast to the arid summit. Here, the Pipiwai (PEE-pee-wy) Trail leads through a dense bamboo forest to the 400-foot Waimoku (wy-MOH-koo) Falls, one of Maui's tallest and most impressive waterfalls. The trail meanders past banyan trees, rushing streams, and towering bamboo that creaks and sways in the wind, creating a soundscape that feels both peaceful and wild. The dramatic plunge of Waimoku Falls into a rocky pool is a fitting finale to the hike, showcasing the lush, verdant beauty of the park's coastal rainforest.

Another highlight of the Kīpahulu District is the Pools of 'Oheʻo, cascading waterfalls and tranquil pools flowing through the forest and into the sea. Known colloquially as the Seven Sacred Pools, these natural swimming holes are a popular spot for visitors to cool off and enjoy the scenery, though swimming is sometimes restricted due to safety concerns. The pools, framed by lush vegetation and volcanic rock, offer a serene setting that feels far removed from the bustling beaches of Maui.

## Hidden Gems: Lesser-Known Spots Worth Exploring

While the summit and coastal areas draw the most attention, Haleakalā National Park is also home to lesser-known spots that offer solitude and a deeper connection to the park's diverse landscapes. One such hidden gem is the Halemauʻu (hah-leh-MA-oo-oo) Trail, which begins near the crater rim and descends through a series of switchbacks into the cloud forest below. The trail offers stunning views of the crater and the surrounding landscape. The dramatic switchback section, the "Rainbow Bridge," provides a particularly photogenic vantage point. The descent into the crater is steep, but the journey through the changing ecosystems—from arid desert to lush forest—is a rewarding experience that showcases the park's incredible diversity.

Another quiet retreat is Hosmer Grove, a short nature trail located just inside the park's entrance near the summit. This area, once planted with non-native trees in an ill-fated forestry experiment, has become a haven for native birds such as the 'iʻiwi (ee-EE-vee) and 'apapane (ah-pah-PAH-neh), which flit among the flowering 'ōhiʻa (oh-HEE-ah) trees. The trail provides a peaceful walk through a mix of native and introduced vegetation, offering birdwatchers a chance to spot some of Hawaii's rarest avian species in a quiet, easily accessible setting.

Visiting the Leleiwi (leh-leh-EE-vee) Overlook provides a less crowded alternative to the main summit for those looking to explore the park's volcanic history. Perched on the crater's rim, this viewpoint offers sweeping views of the cinder cones and lava fields below, framed by twisted, gnarled māmane (MAH-mah-neh) trees. The overlook is breathtaking in the late afternoon when the setting sun casts a warm glow over the landscape, highlighting the vibrant reds and oranges of the crater floor.

## Hiking Trails

Haleakalā's hiking trails offer an array of experiences, from short walks through lush rainforests to strenuous treks across barren volcanic landscapes.

### *Sliding Sands Trail*

Length: 11 miles (17.7 km) round-trip
Elevation Change: 2,800 feet (853 meters)
Difficulty: Strenuous

The Sliding Sands Trail is one of the most iconic hikes in Haleakalā, offering a challenging journey into the heart of the crater. The trail begins at the summit and descends steeply, passing through a landscape of vivid cinder cones, lava fields, and rare silversword plants. The stark beauty of the trail is mesmerizing, with each turn revealing new colors and textures that tell the story of the volcano's turbulent past. While the descent is relatively easy, the return climb is strenuous, requiring hikers to navigate steep switchbacks and endure the high-altitude conditions. This hike is best attempted early in the day to avoid the midday heat and ensure a safe return.

*Halemau'u (hah-leh-MA-oo-oo) Trail to Holua (hoh-LOO-ah) Cabin*

Length: 7.4 miles (11.9 km) round-trip
Elevation Change: 1,000 feet (305 meters)
Difficulty: Moderate

The Halemau'u Trail offers a more moderate alternative to the Sliding Sands Trail, with stunning views of the crater and the surrounding landscape. The trail begins at a scenic overlook and descends through a series of switchbacks known for their dramatic views and steep drop-offs. The trail levels out as it enters the crater, leading hikers through a surreal landscape of lava flows, cinder cones, and desert vegetation. The turnaround point is the Holua Cabin, a rustic shelter that provides a picturesque spot to rest and enjoy the quiet beauty of the crater. The return journey is a steady climb back to the rim, with the changing light providing new perspectives on the volcanic landscape.

*Pipiwai (pee-pee-why) Trail to Waimoku (Why-moh-koo) Falls*

Length: 4 miles (6.4 km) round-trip
Elevation Change: 800 feet (244 meters)
Difficulty: Moderate

Located in the Kīpahulu (kee-pah-HOO-loo) District, the Pipiwai Trail is a must-do for visitors seeking a lush, tropical hiking experience. The trail winds through dense bamboo forests, past ancient banyan trees, and alongside cascading streams, creating a vibrant, jungle-like atmosphere. The final stretch of the trail leads to Waimoku (wy-MOH-koo) Falls, a stunning 400-foot waterfall that plunges down a sheer cliff into a rocky pool below. The sight of the falls, framed by lush vegetation and the sound of rushing water, creates a serene and awe-inspiring setting. The trail's moderate difficulty and scenic beauty make it one of the most popular hikes in the park.

*Homers Grove Nature Trail*

Length: 0.5 miles (0.8 km) loop
Elevation Change: Minimal
Difficulty: Easy

The Hosmer Grove Nature Trail offers a short, peaceful walk through a unique mix of native and non-native trees, providing a glimpse into the park's diverse ecosystems. The trail is a favorite among birdwatchers, as it offers the chance to spot some of Hawaii's rarest forest birds, including the bright red 'i'iwi (ee-ee-vee) and the 'apapane (ah-pah-pah-neh). Interpretive signs along the trail provide insights into the park's flora and fauna, making it an educational and enjoyable experience for visitors of all ages.

## Other Activities: Beyond the Trails – Experiencing Haleakalā's Unique Wonders

Beyond hiking, Haleakalā National Park offers a variety of activities that highlight its stunning landscapes and rich cultural significance.

*Stargazing at the Summit*

Stargazing at the summit of Haleakalā is one of the park's most enchanting activities, drawing visitors worldwide to experience the breathtaking night sky. The high elevation (over 10,000 feet) and minimal light pollution create ideal conditions for astronomical observations. On clear nights, the view is nothing short of spectacular, with thousands of stars twinkling brightly, distant planets shimmering, and the Milky Way stretching across the sky in a dazzling display. The summit's observatories, used for scientific research, enhance the experience, allowing amateur astronomers and enthusiasts alike to gain insights into the universe. Many visitors join ranger-led stargazing programs to learn about celestial navigation and the myths and legends associated with the stars in Hawaiian culture. As you gaze into the vastness of the night sky, the experience becomes a profound reminder of your place in the cosmos.

### *Biking Down Haleakalā*

For those seeking adventure, biking down Haleakalā's summit offers a thrilling way to explore the park. Several guided tours provide the opportunity to descend from the crater's rim to the coast, taking cyclists through a remarkable range of ecosystems. The ride begins at the summit in a stark, barren landscape, where the unique volcanic terrain sets the stage for what lies ahead. As you descend, the scenery transforms dramatically, revealing lush tropical landscapes filled with vibrant flowers, rolling pastures, and verdant valleys. The exhilarating descent, often accompanied by sweeping views of the coastline and neighboring islands, is an unforgettable experience. Cyclists can stop along the way to take in the views, snap photos, and enjoy the fresh mountain air, making it a perfect blend of adventure and natural beauty.

### *Cultural Programs and Experiences*

Engaging in cultural programs led by Native Hawaiian rangers gives visitors a deep understanding of Haleakalā's significance to the Hawaiian people. These programs encompass traditional Hawaiian chants, storytelling, and demonstrations of cultural practices such as hula and lei making. Participants are encouraged to immerse themselves in the rich history and traditions associated with the land. Through these experiences, visitors can gain insight into the Hawaiian people's deep connection with Haleakalā, learning about its spiritual significance, legends, and the importance of stewardship. This cultural exchange fosters a greater appreciation for the land and its people, encouraging respectful interactions and ongoing efforts to preserve this heritage.

## *Wildlife Watching*

Haleakalā is also home to a variety of unique wildlife, making it an excellent destination for nature enthusiasts. The park's diverse ecosystems support species such as the endangered Hawaiian goose (nene), the monk seal, and numerous native bird species. Early mornings or late afternoons are the best times for wildlife watching, as many animals are more active during these cooler hours. Join a ranger-led wildlife program to learn more about the park's inhabitants and their habitats, as well as ongoing conservation efforts aimed at protecting these vulnerable species. Observing wildlife in their natural environment adds an extra layer of excitement and connection to the landscape.

## *Camping Under the Stars*

Camping at Haleakalā National Park allows you to fully immerse yourself in its natural beauty and enjoy the tranquility of the wilderness. The park offers several campgrounds, including Hosmer Grove and the Kipahulu area, where you can set up your tent amidst native plants and the sounds of nature. As night falls, the clear skies provide excellent stargazing opportunities, allowing you to see constellations and celestial events with stunning clarity. The experience of falling asleep under a blanket of stars, surrounded by the peaceful sounds of the forest, is a cherished memory for many visitors.

## Flora and Fauna: The Park's Diverse Ecosystems

Haleakalā National Park is home to some of the world's most unique and diverse ecosystems, ranging from arid volcanic landscapes to lush rainforests filled with endemic species. The summit of Haleakalā is characterized by its stark, desert-like environment, where hardy plants like the silversword cling to life among the cinders and lava rocks. The silversword, a rare and endangered plant that blooms once before dying, is one of the park's most iconic species, with its silvery leaves and tall, flowering stalks creating a striking contrast against the volcanic terrain.

The park's lower elevations are home to lush rainforests filled with native plants and animals found nowhere else on Earth. The Kīpahulu District, with its dense bamboo forests and towering waterfalls, supports a rich array of flora, including 'ōhi'a lehua (Oh-hee-ah Leh-hoo-ah) trees, ferns, and flowering vines. The forests are also home to native birds such as the 'amakihi (ah-mah-KEE-hee) and 'i'iwi, which can be seen flitting among the treetops in flashes of yellow and red.

The park's coastal areas, where the mountains meet the sea, provide critical habitat for endangered species such as the Hawaiian monk seal and the nēnē, Hawaii's state bird. The pools, streams, and waterfalls of the Kīpahulu District support a variety of native fish and invertebrates, highlighting the interconnectedness of the park's diverse ecosystems.

## Best Campgrounds and Accommodation Options

Camping in Haleakalā National Park offers a unique opportunity to experience the park's diverse landscapes up close. Hosmer Grove Campground, located near the summit, is a small, rustic campground nestled among trees at an elevation of 7,000 feet. The campground provides easy access to the summit trails. It offers a cool, quiet retreat with stunning views of the surrounding mountains. Nights can be chilly, but the clear, star-filled skies make it a perfect spot for stargazing.

The Kīpahulu Campground, located in the park's coastal district, offers a more tropical camping experience. Its sites are surrounded by lush vegetation and close to the park's waterfalls and pools. The campground provides easy access to the Pipiwai Trail and the Pools of 'Ohe'o, making it a convenient base for exploring the park's rainforest and coastal areas.

For those seeking indoor accommodations, there are no lodges within Haleakalā National Park, but nearby towns such as Hana offer a range of options, from charming bed and breakfasts to luxury resorts. Staying in Hana allows visitors to explore the park's coastal district while enjoying the comfort of a warm bed and local Hawaiian hospitality.

## Mysterious Sightings: UFO Encounters Over Haleakalā National Park

### UFO Sightings Over the Crater

In the summer of 2016, several visitors to Haleakalā National Park reported a series of unusual sightings over the volcanic crater that sparked intrigue and speculation. During a particularly clear night, a group of stargazers gathered at the summit to take in the breath-taking views of the night sky. The area, known for its minimal light pollution, is a prime location for stargazing, but that evening, something else caught their attention.

As they admired the stars, one group member noticed a series of bright, pulsating lights moving erratically above the crater. Initially, they assumed it was an airplane, but the lights did not follow a conventional flight path. Instead, they hovered, darted, and changed colors, shifting from bright white to deep red and green in an almost mesmerizing display.

The group quickly grabbed their phones and began filming, hoping to capture evidence of what they were witnessing. As they recorded, the lights began to form distinct patterns, moving in unison as if choreographed. Other visitors at the summit joined in, pointing and gasping in disbelief.

One of the witnesses, an amateur astronomer, speculated that what they were seeing might not be of earthly origin. "It was like nothing I've ever seen before," he later recounted. "The way those lights moved—it defied logic. I've watched countless satellites and planes, but this was different. It felt almost intentional."

As word spread, more visitors arrived, drawn by the commotion. Intrigued by the reports, local park rangers decided to investigate. They later confirmed that no scheduled flights were in the area that night, and the weather conditions were clear, ruling out mete-orological phenomena.

While some skeptics dismissed the sightings as mere drones or military aircraft, the visitors remained convinced they had witnessed something extraordinary. The event sparked discussions in local forums and social media, with many sharing similar experiences from past visits to Haleakalā, leading to speculation about UFOs and extraterrestrial visitors to the volcanic landscape.

## The 1970s Military Sightings

In the late 1970s, several members of the U.S. Air Force stationed on the island reported sightings of strange lights near Haleakalā. These lights were described as bright orbs that moved rapidly across the sky, often changing direction abruptly. Some airmen claimed to have observed these phenomena while conducting routine training exercises, and their accounts were documented in local military records. Although some dismissed the sightings as military aircraft, others speculated about the possibility of unidentified flying objects.

## The 1992 Family Encounter

In 1992, a family visiting Haleakalā reported a strange encounter while camping in the park. One night, as they sat around their campfire, they noticed a series of flashing lights hovering above the crater. The lights appeared to pulse in different colors and then suddenly shot off into the distance. The family members were initially startled and confused, and they later reported their experience to park rangers, who documented the sighting. The family maintained that they had witnessed something inexplicable, fueling discussions about potential extraterrestrial activity in the area.

## The 2004 Sunset Sighting

A group of tourists visiting Haleakalā at sunset in 2004 reported seeing unusual objects in the sky after the sun dipped below the horizon. Descriptions varied, with some witnesses describing them as cigar-shaped crafts. In contrast, others noted bright orbs dancing across the sky. The sighting garnered attention when multiple visitors independently reported the phenomenon to the park's visitor center. Park staff noted the reports but could not confirm any logical explanation for the lights, leaving the mystery unresolved.

## Practical Travel Tips and Planning Information

Haleakalā is best visited in the early morning or late afternoon to avoid the midday heat and to catch the dramatic light that transforms the landscape. If you plan to watch the sunrise from the summit, be sure to make a reservation in advance, as spots fill up quickly. Dress warmly, as temperatures at the summit can be below freezing, even in summer, and bring a flashlight to navigate the rocky paths before dawn.

The drive to the summit is steep and winding, so take your time and enjoy the scenic pullouts along the way. Be prepared for rapidly changing weather, as clouds can roll in suddenly, obscuring the views. At the Kīpahulu District, bring water and sturdy shoes for hiking, as the trails can be muddy and slippery, especially after rain.

Respect the park's cultural and ecological significance by staying on designated trails, avoiding touching or disturbing the native plants, and following Leave No Trace principles. The park's ecosystems are fragile and irreplaceable, and your actions can help preserve them for future generations.

## Conclusion: Inspiring Further Exploration

Haleakalā National Park is a place of contrasts and wonder, where the power of nature is on full display. Haleakalā invites you to explore, reflect, and connect with the land's ancient spirit, from the windswept summit that touches the sky to the lush rainforests and cascading waterfalls. This is a place where legends come to life, where every sunrise feels like a gift, and where the resilience of nature is celebrated in every bloom and birdcall.

As you leave the park, take with you the sense of awe and reverence that Haleakalā inspires. Whether you're watching the sunrise from the summit, hiking through the crater's cinder fields, or listening to the rush of waterfalls in the rainforest, let the park's beauty and cultural heritage remind you of the importance of protecting these wild places. Haleakalā's story is one of creation, adaptation, and endurance—a story that continues to unfold with every sunrise and every step you take on its sacred ground.

# NINE

# Hawai'i Volcanoes National Park

## THE LAND OF FIRE AND CREATION

 *"In the heart of the volcano, we find the spirit of the islands."*

Unknown

### Introduction: The Park's History and Significance

Hawai'i Volcanoes National Park is a dynamic landscape of fire, lava, and rebirth, where two of the world's most active volcanoes— Kīlauea (kee-lau-WEH-ah) and Mauna Loa (MOW-nah LOH-ah)—continuously shape and reshape the island of Hawai'i. This land, marked by molten lava flows, steaming vents, and ancient rainforests, tells the ongoing story of the Earth's creation, where land is born from fire, and the forces of nature are on full display. For centuries, the volcanoes have been revered and respected by Native Hawaiians, who see them as the home of Pele, the Hawaiian goddess of fire, lightning, wind, and volcanoes.

The cultural and spiritual significance of Kīlauea and Mauna Loa runs deep in Hawaiian tradition. According to legend, Pele makes her home in Halema'uma'u (hah-leh-MAU-mah-oo) Crater at the summit of Kīlauea, where her presence can be felt in the glowing lava lake and the billowing plumes of volcanic gas that rise from the crater. For Native Hawaiians, these volcanoes are more than geological features; they are living, breathing

entities that command respect and reverence. Ancient chants, myths, and hula dances tell of Pele's fiery temper and her power to create and destroy, embodying the dual nature of the volcanoes that both devastate and give birth to new land.

The first recorded European observation of Kīlauea occurred in 1823 when missionary Reverend William Ellis and a group of explorers ventured into the crater, describing it as a "subterranean world of fire." The explorers marveled at the sight of molten lava bubbling and flowing, an image that left a lasting impression and drew scientists, adventurers, and artists to the island in the following decades. Among them was Mark Twain, who visited the volcano in 1866 and described it as "a scene of wild beauty," capturing the imagination of readers worldwide.

Hawai'i Volcanoes National Park was established in 1916, making it one of the oldest national parks in the United States. The park was created to protect the unique volcanic landscapes, endemic plant and animal species, and cultural sites that define the area. Over the years, the park has expanded to include over 330,000 acres of diverse terrain, ranging from the summit of Mauna Loa, the world's largest volcano, to the rugged coastline where lava meets the sea.

Today, the park is recognized as a UNESCO World Heritage Site and an International Biosphere Reserve, highlighting its global importance as a living geological laboratory and a sanctuary for rare and endangered species. Conservation efforts within the park focus on managing invasive species, restoring native habitats, and preserving the cultural heritage of the Hawaiian people. Kīlauea's frequent eruptions offer a powerful reminder of the island's volcanic origins and the ongoing forces that continue to shape the land. As you explore Hawai'i Volcanoes National Park, you are walking on the newest land on Earth—a landscape that is constantly evolving, changing, and creating.

## Fascinating Facts About Hawai'i Volcanoes National Park

1. **Active Volcanoes:** The park is home to two of the world's most active volcanoes, Kīlauea and Mauna Loa.
2. **Formation:** The park was established in 1961 to protect the unique volcanic landscape and ecosystems.
3. **Geothermal Features:** The park features numerous geothermal areas, including steam vents, sulfur banks, and mud pots.
4. **Lava Tubes:** Lava tubes, like the Thurston Lava Tube, are natural tunnels formed by flowing lava that have cooled and hardened.
5. **Hydrothermal Explosions:** The park has experienced hydrothermal explosions, which occur when water is heated by volcanic activity and rapidly turns to steam.
6. **Cultural Significance:** The park is sacred to Native Hawaiians, who believe the volcano goddess Pele resides in Kīlauea.
7. **Diverse Ecosystems:** The park encompasses diverse ecosystems, from lush rainforests to barren volcanic landscapes.

1. **Mauna Loa Observatory:** The observatory on Mauna Loa is a key site for studying atmospheric carbon dioxide levels.
2. **Pele's Hair**: Thin strands of volcanic glass, known as Pele's hair, can be found in the park, formed from lava fountains.
3. **Historic Eruptions:** Kīlauea has been erupting intermittently since 1983, with the most recent activity occurring in 2018.

## Key Highlights and Must-See Landmarks

Hawai'i Volcanoes National Park is a place of endless fascination, where every visit offers a chance to witness the raw power of volcanic activity and explore the park's diverse and dramatic landscapes. One of the park's most iconic landmarks is the Kīlauea Caldera, a massive, sunken crater that stretches nearly three miles across and is home to Halema'uma'u (Hah-leh-mah-oo-mah-oo) Crater, the fiery heart of the volcano. At Halema'uma'u, Pele's spirit is said to reside, and the sight of molten lava glowing within the crater, especially at night, is a breathtaking reminder of the Earth's untamed power.

A drive along Crater Rim Drive offers numerous viewpoints and overlooks that provide stunning vistas of Kīlauea's dynamic landscape. The Jaggar Museum Overlook is one of the best spots to view the caldera and the ongoing volcanic activity within Halema'uma'u Crater. Through interactive exhibits, visitors can learn about the park's geology, volcanic history, and the cultural significance of the volcanoes. On clear nights, the museum's overlook offers a spectacular view of the lava lake's glow, illuminating the surrounding landscape with an eerie red light.

The Chain of Craters Road is another must-see, winding its way from the summit of Kīlauea down to the coast, where lava flows have repeatedly reshaped the landscape. The road passes by numerous volcanic features, including pit craters, old lava flows, and steam vents. At the end of the road, visitors can witness the dramatic meeting of lava and ocean, where molten rock pours into the sea, sending up billows of steam and creating new land before your eyes. This powerful spectacle of creation is a reminder of the park's ever-changing nature and the relentless forces that shape the Hawaiian Islands.

One of the park's most unique attractions is the Thurston Lava Tube, a massive, hollow tunnel formed by a molten lava river flowing beneath the surface thousands of years ago. Walking through the lava tube is like stepping into another world, where the walls glisten with mineral deposits, and the air is cool and damp. The short hike through the tube and the surrounding lush rainforest provides a fascinating glimpse into the park's volcanic processes and the interplay between fire and life.

The summit of Mauna Loa, the world's largest active volcano, is another highlight for intrepid explorers. While reaching the summit is a challenging endeavor requiring a multi-day hike through rugged terrain, the experience is unlike any other. The summit's vast, windswept crater feels like the surface of another planet, with its barren, rocky landscape and thin, crisp air. On a clear day, the view from the summit stretches across the island, offering a bird's-eye perspective on the volcanic forces that have shaped Hawai'i for millennia.

## Hidden Gems: Lesser-Known Spots Worth Exploring

Beyond the popular viewpoints and landmarks, Hawai'i Volcanoes National Park is filled with hidden gems that offer quieter, more intimate encounters with the park's volcanic and natural wonders. One such spot is the Pu'u Loa (POO-oo LOH-ah) Petroglyphs, an ancient site on the park's southern coast where thousands of petroglyphs tell the stories of the Native Hawaiians who once lived here. The petroglyphs, etched into the hardened lava, depict human figures, canoes, and symbols of the natural world, providing a fascinating glimpse into the cultural heritage of the Hawaiian people. A short hike along a boardwalk trail leads visitors to the petroglyph field, where the carvings are preserved amid the stark, black lava.

Another hidden treasure is the Kīlauea Iki (kee-lau-WEH-ah EE-kee) Trail, a 4-mile loop that descends from the lush rainforest into the crater of a 1959 eruption. The trail begins at the crater's rim, winding through dense ferns and ʻōhiʻa (oh-HEE-ah) trees before dropping onto the solidified lava lake below. Walking across the crater floor, with its cracked surface and steaming vents, is like stepping onto another planet. The trail offers an up-close look at the powerful forces that shaped this landscape, and the contrast between the vibrant forest and the barren crater floor highlights the park's dynamic nature.

The Mauna Ulu Trail offers a quieter alternative to the busier summit areas, leading hikers through a landscape of recent lava flows, cinder cones, and tree molds created when lava engulfed the trunks of living trees. The trail's endpoint, the summit of Mauna Ulu, provides panoramic views of Kīlauea's East Rift Zone and the surrounding volcanic landscape. The area's relatively recent eruptions, which occurred from 1969 to 1974, have left behind a landscape still in the early stages of recovery, offering a unique opportunity to witness the beginnings of new life taking hold in the volcanic rock.

# Hiking Trails

Hawai'i Volcanoes National Park's hiking trails allow visitors to explore the park's diverse environments, from lush rainforests to barren lava fields.

## *Kīlauea Iki Trail*

Length: 4 miles (6.4 km) loop
Elevation Change: 400 feet (122 meters)
Difficulty: Moderate

The Kīlauea Iki Trail is a favorite among visitors, offering a stunning journey from the rainforest to the crater floor of a once-roaring lava lake. The trail begins at the crater's rim, descending through a lush forest filled with ferns, orchids, and native 'ōhi'a trees before emerging onto the solidified lava lake below. As you walk across the crater floor, the landscape shifts from lush green to stark black, with steam vents releasing wisps of sulfur-scented gas. The trail is marked by cairns, guiding hikers across the cracked surface of the lava lake, which still bears the marks of the 1959 eruption. The contrast between the vibrant forest and the barren crater is striking, showcasing the park's ever-evolving nature.

## *Devastation Trail*

Length: 1 mile (1.6 km) round-trip
Elevation Change: Minimal
Difficulty: Easy

The Devastation Trail offers a short, easy walk through an area buried by cinders and ash during a 1959 eruption of Kīlauea Iki.

The trail is paved and accessible, making it a great option for families and those looking for a quick, educational hike. Along the trail, interpretive signs provide insights into the eruption and its impact on the surrounding landscape, where native plants are slowly beginning to reclaim the barren ground. The eerie, moon-like terrain is a stark reminder of the power of volcanic activity and the slow but steady process of ecological recovery.

### Pu'u Loa (Poo-oo- Loh-ah) Petroglyphs Trail

Length: 1.4 miles (2.3 km) round-trip
Elevation Change: Minimal
Difficulty: Easy

This short, relatively flat trail leads to the Pu'u Loa Petroglyph Field, one of Hawaii's largest and most significant petroglyph sites. The trail meanders through a landscape of rugged lava flows, where thousands of ancient carvings tell the stories of Native Hawaiians who once lived on this land. The petroglyphs include images of people, animals, canoes, and other symbols etched into the lava rock over centuries. A raised boardwalk lets visitors view the petroglyphs up close while protecting this cultural treasure. The trail offers a unique glimpse into the history and traditions of the Hawaiian people, connecting the modern visitor to the island's ancient past.

### Mauna Ulu Trail

Length: 2.5 miles (4 km) round-trip
Elevation Change: 210 feet (64 meters)
Difficulty: Moderate

The Mauna Ulu Trail takes hikers on a journey through a landscape shaped by recent volcanic activity. The trail winds through lava fields, tree molds, and cinder cones, providing a fascinating look at the volcanic processes that have shaped the park. The trail's highlight is the summit of Mauna Ulu, a vent that erupted continuously for five years, creating a dramatic landscape of lava flows and volcanic features. The summit offers sweeping views of the East Rift Zone and the surrounding lava fields, providing a unique perspective on the park's ongoing geological activity.

## Other Activities: Beyond the Trails – Experiencing Hawai'i Volcanoes' Fiery Wonders

Beyond hiking, Hawai'i Volcanoes National Park offers many activities that showcase its unique volcanic landscapes and rich cultural heritage.

### *Ranger-Led Programs*

Ranger-led programs are an excellent way to deepen your understanding of the park's geology, ecology, and the cultural significance of its volcanoes. These programs include guided walks, educational talks, and interactive demonstrations highlighting the park's dynamic environment. For example, a ranger may lead a hike through an old lava flow, explaining how the land was formed and discussing the fascinating plant and animal adaptations that have evolved in this volcanic landscape. Visitors can also learn about the cultural stories of the Hawaiian people, including the mythology surrounding the volcanoes and their importance in Hawaiian identity. Engaging with knowledgeable rangers provides a rich context for your visit and fosters a greater appreciation for the natural wonders of the park.

## *Guided Lava Tours*

For those seeking an up-close look at the park's volcanic activity, guided lava tours offer the chance to witness active lava flows (when conditions permit). Led by experienced guides, these tours take visitors to areas where lava is actively creating new land, providing a once-in-a-lifetime opportunity to see the Earth in the creation process. As you stand on the hardened lava, watching the molten rock flow and solidify, you'll experience the raw power of nature firsthand. The sight of glowing lava, especially as the sun sets, is both humbling and exhilarating, a vivid reminder of the powerful forces that continue to shape the Hawaiian Islands. Many tour guides share personal stories and scientific insights, making the experience even more memorable.

## *Stargazing*

Stargazing is another popular activity at Hawai'i Volcanoes, as the park's high elevation and remote location provide excellent conditions for viewing the night sky. The summit of Mauna Loa offers particularly stunning vantage points, where visitors can see the Milky Way, distant planets, and shooting stars in crystal-clear detail. On clear nights, the glow of Kīlauea's lava lake can be seen in the distance, adding a fiery glow to the celestial display. Ranger-led stargazing programs often accompany these clear nights, where you can learn about the constellations, the stories behind them, and the cultural significance of the night sky to Hawaiian culture. Bringing a telescope or binoculars enhances the experience, allowing you to explore the universe's wonders.

## Cultural Experiences

Hawai'i Volcanoes National Park offers a variety of cultural experiences that celebrate the rich heritage of the Hawaiian people. Participants can participate in workshops that teach traditional Hawaiian practices, such as hula dancing, lei making, and crafting with native plants. These experiences provide a deeper connection to the land and its history, allowing visitors to appreciate the traditions that have been passed down through generations. Engaging with local artisans and cultural practitioners can offer insights into the importance of these practices and their connection to the park's natural resources.

## Wildlife Watching

The diverse ecosystems within the park support a rich array of wildlife, making wildlife watching an exciting activity. Keep an eye out for native species such as the Hawaiian 'elepaio (eh-leh-PY-oh), a forest bird known for its distinctive calls, or the endangered Hawaiian goose (nene), which can often be seen grazing in the park. The habitats, from lush rainforests to volcanic landscapes, provide opportunities to observe wildlife in different settings. Early mornings and late afternoons are the best times for sightings, and joining a ranger-led wildlife program can enhance your understanding of the animals and their behaviors.

## Photography

Photography enthusiasts will find countless opportunities to capture the breathtaking landscapes and vibrant ecosystems of Hawai'i Volcanoes. The dramatic contrast of lush green rainforests against the stark black lava flows creates striking images. Popular spots for photography include the Jaggar Museum overlook, where you can capture the glow of Kīlauea's lava lake, and the Thurston Lava Tube, which offers a unique perspective on the park's volcanic history.

## Flora and Fauna: The Park's Diverse Ecosystems

Hawai'i Volcanoes National Park is home to a rich array of ecosystems, ranging from barren lava fields to lush rainforests teeming with life. The park's unique environment supports a variety of endemic species, including the iconic nēnē (Hawaiian goose), which is found nowhere else in the world. The nēnē, once on the brink of extinction, has made a remarkable recovery thanks to conservation efforts within the park, and visitors can often spot these charming birds waddling along the trails and roadways.

The park's rainforests, located at lower elevations, are filled with native plants such as 'ōhi'a lehua (Oh-hee-ah Leh-hoo-ah), ferns, and bamboo orchids, creating a lush, green contrast to the stark volcanic landscape above. These forests provide a critical habitat for native birds like the 'apapane (ah-pah-PAH-neh) and 'amakihi (Ah-mah-kee-hee), whose bright plumage and melodic calls bring life to the forest canopy. The rainforests also support a variety of unique insects, including the happy face spider, named for the distinct, smiling pattern on its abdomen.

The high-altitude desert of Mauna Loa's summit is a harsh but fascinating environment where only the hardiest plants and animals can survive. The rocky landscape is home to the rare silversword, a spiky, silver-hued plant that blooms only once in its lifetime, and various endemic insects that have adapted to the extreme conditions. The summit's thin air and rugged terrain create a stark, otherworldly landscape that feels far removed from the tropical paradise below.

## Best Campgrounds and Accommodation Options

Camping in Hawai'i Volcanoes National Park offers a unique way to experience the park's dramatic landscapes and volcanic wonders. Nāmakanipaio (NAH-mah-kah-nee-PAH-ee-0h) Campground, located at an elevation of 4,000 feet, offers a cool, forested setting with spacious campsites surrounded by towering eucalyptus and 'ōhi'a trees. The campground is conveniently located near the park's main attractions, making it an ideal base for exploring Kīlauea and the surrounding trails.

For a more remote experience, Kulanaokuaiki (koo-lah-nah-oh-koo-ah-EE-kee) Campground provides a quieter, more rustic alternative. Its sites are nestled among lava flows and native vegetation. This off-the-beaten-path campground offers solitude and stunning views of the volcanic landscape, especially at sunset, when the sky and lava rock glow in shades of red and orange.

Backcountry camping is also available for those seeking an adventure off the beaten path. Permits are required, and hikers should be prepared for rugged conditions and rapidly changing weather. Popular backcountry sites include campsites along the Mauna Loa Trail, where campers can experience the stark beauty of the summit firsthand.

## Mysterious Sightings and Encounters at Hawai'i Volcanoes National Park

### *The Ghost of Kīlauea*

The legend of the Ghost of Kīlauea has fascinated visitors for generations. According to local lore, the ghost is said to be the spirit of a young Hawaiian woman who tragically lost her life during a volcanic eruption in the late 1800s. Her family, unable to escape the lava flow, perished in the fiery chaos, and her spirit has been said to wander the volcanic terrain ever since.

Many who visit Kīlauea have reported seeing her apparition, often described as a figure clad in flowing white garments. Witnesses claim that she appears near the edge of the caldera, where the ground trembles and the air is thick with sulfur. Some visitors have recounted feeling an inexplicable chill in the air or experiencing sudden gusts of wind when she is near.

Park rangers have documented numerous accounts from visitors who describe their encounters in vivid detail. One hiker recalled, "As I approached the caldera at sunset, I saw a figure in white standing at the edge. At first, I thought it was a fellow hiker, but when I got closer, she vanished into thin air." Such encounters often leave a lasting impression, instilling both awe and a sense of connection to the park's rich history and cultural heritage.

The ghostly presence has become a topic of interest for park-goers and paranormal enthusiasts, leading to organized ghost tours and storytelling sessions highlighting the blend of natural beauty and cultural stories within Hawaiʻi Volcanoes National Park.

### The "Pele's Hair" Lights

Another intriguing report came from a group of campers who claimed to see glowing strands resembling "Pele's hair" floating above the lava fields. The glowing strands reportedly moved as if alive, weaving through the air before vanishing. While scientists believe this could be explained by glowing volcanic glass particles, the sighting remains a captivating story among park visitors, often shared around campfires.

## Practical Travel Tips and Planning Information

Hawai'i Volcanoes is best visited in the early morning or late afternoon to avoid the midday crowds and catch the dramatic lighting that transforms the volcanic landscape. If you plan to visit the summit areas, be sure to bring warm layers, as temperatures can be surprisingly cold, even in summer. The park's high elevations and variable weather mean that conditions can change rapidly, so be prepared for rain, wind, and even snow at the summit of Mauna Loa.

The Chain of Craters Road is a must-do, but be sure to check for road closures, as lava flows can sometimes block access. If you plan to see active lava flows, be aware that conditions change frequently, and safety is paramount. Always stay on marked trails, keep a safe distance, and heed any warnings or closures. Bring plenty of water and sunscreen, as the volcanic landscape offers little shade, and the sun can be intense.

Respect the park's cultural and natural heritage by following Leave No Trace principles, staying on designated trails, and avoiding disturbing the native plants and wildlife. The park's ecosystems are delicate and easily impacted, so your efforts to protect them help ensure that this land of fire and creation remains for future generations.

## Conclusion: Inspiring Further Exploration

Hawai'i Volcanoes National Park is a place of extraordinary beauty and raw power, where the forces of fire and time constantly shape and reshape the land. From the fiery glow of Kīlauea's lava lake to the quiet solitude of the Mauna Loa summit, the park offers a profound connection to the Earth's ancient processes and the rich cultural heritage of the Hawaiian people. This is a place where creation and destruction exist side by side, and every step you take on its volcanic terrain is a journey through the ongoing story of the land.

Let the park's dynamic landscapes inspire you to explore, learn, and appreciate the delicate balance of life in a place shaped by some of the most powerful forces on Earth. Whether walking through a lava tube, watching the sunrise from the crater rim, or simply standing in awe of the lava's fiery glow, Hawai'i Volcanoes invites you to connect with the natural world in a deeply meaningful way. The park's ever-changing nature is a reminder of the land's resilience and the Hawaiian Islands' enduring spirit—an invitation to witness the miracle of creation in real-time.

# Conclusion

## THE PACIFIC'S TIMELESS BEAUTY AND THE JOURNEY AHEAD

As we conclude this journey through the Pacific's most breathtaking national parks, it becomes clear that these lands are more than just beautiful places—they are living stories of our planet's history, natural wonders that speak of time, resilience, and the enduring spirit of the wild. From the towering redwoods that have stood sentinel for millennia to the dynamic, lava-sculpted landscapes of Hawai'i Volcanoes, each park invites us to pause, breathe, and reconnect with the natural world in an increasingly rare way.

These parks are not just destinations; they are reminders of the importance of preserving the natural wonders that shape our world. Whether you're standing on the windswept summit of Haleakalā, hiking through the lush rainforests of Olympic, or gazing into the sapphire depths of Crater Lake, these experiences leave an indelible mark. They teach us to appreciate the land's power and beauty, respect the delicate balance of ecosystems, and protect these wild places for future generations.

Our exploration also reveals the mysterious encounters reported by visitors—stories that add an intriguing layer to the parks' narratives. From unexplained lights in the sky to ghostly figures on the trails, these accounts remind us that nature holds many secrets yet to be discovered.

Our exploration of the Pacific region is just the beginning of a more extensive journey that will take us to the towering peaks, expansive deserts, and hidden valleys of other incredible national parks across the United States. In the upcoming books of this series, we will venture into the Rocky Mountain region, exploring the rugged beauty of parks like Yellowstone, Grand Teton, and Rocky Mountain National Park. These landscapes will offer new adventures, with each park showcasing its unique blend of natural wonders, wildlife, and history.

We will also explore the Southwest's iconic red rock formations, deep canyons, and ancient cultural sites in parks like Zion, Grand Canyon, and Arches. This region's dramatic scenery and rich cultural heritage tell the story of a land shaped by water, wind, and the passage of time. You'll learn about the ancient peoples who once called these landscapes home and the conservation efforts that continue to protect these fragile environments.

As we move eastward, we'll explore the serene and biodiverse parks of the Great Lakes and Appalachian regions. Here, lush forests, cascading waterfalls, and quiet mountain trails offer a completely different yet equally captivating experience of America's natural heritage. These parks, such as the Great Smoky Mountains and Shenandoah, will highlight the ecological diversity and historical significance of the nation's eastern landscapes.

Each book in this series will follow the same thoughtful approach, blending vivid storytelling with practical tips and insights to help you plan your adventures. You'll find a mix of well-known highlights and hidden gems. Whether you're a seasoned adventurer or just beginning your journey into the wild, these books are designed to inspire, educate, and encourage you to explore the vast and varied beauty of America's national parks.

National parks are often called "America's best idea," and with good reason. They protect our natural and cultural treasures, offer refuge for wildlife, and provide a place for us to escape, recharge, and find inspiration in the simple, profound beauty of the natural world. As you continue your journey, may these parks remind you of the power of nature, the importance of conservation, and the joy that comes from discovering the world's wild places.

Thank you for joining me in exploring the Pacific region's national parks. I hope this book has inspired you to visit these incredible places and deepened your appreciation for the landscapes that define the American West. There's so much more to see and stories to tell.

I look forward to continuing this journey with you as we explore the next breathtaking chapters of America's great outdoors.

Let's keep exploring, protecting, and finding wonder in the natural world. The journey has only just begun.

# Pacific Wonders: Exploring the National Parks

Now that you've journeyed through the breathtaking landscapes and hidden treasures of the Pacific region's national parks, it's time to share your experiences and guide others to these natural wonders.

Your adventure through *Pacific Wonders* has equipped you with insights into the geological history, unique wildlife, and awe-inspiring trails of each park. You've discovered serene coastal vistas, ancient forests, and volcanic marvels that define these special places. Now, you have the power to help others find the same sense of wonder and inspiration.

By leaving a review, you can:

- Help a nature enthusiast discover the magic of the Pacific parks.
- Support a traveler in planning their next unforgettable outdoor adventure.
- Encourage another reader to explore the natural beauty and hidden gems within these parks.

Your review doesn't just capture your thoughts—it becomes a guiding light for others eager to explore the wilderness. It can inspire, motivate, and provide the reassurance that they too can experience the joys of these stunning landscapes.

So, if this book has enriched your journey through the Pacific's natural wonders, please take a moment to share your experience.

Your words could be the nudge that someone else needs to begin their adventure.

Simply scan the QR code below to leave your review:

Thank you for being part of this exploration. Your insights and feedback mean the world to me and to the many adventurers who will follow in your footsteps.

**Your fellow explorer,**

- Everett Wilder

# References

National Park Service. (n.d.). *Yosemite National Park*. U.S. Department of the Interior. Retrieved from https://www.nps.gov/yose/index.htm

National Park Service. (n.d.). *Sequoia & Kings Canyon National Parks*. U.S. Department of the Interior. Retrieved from https://www.nps.gov/seki/index.htm

National Park Service. (n.d.). *Joshua Tree National Park*. U.S. Department of the Interior. Retrieved from https://www.nps.gov/jotr/index.htm

National Park Service. (n.d.). *Redwood National and State Parks*. U.S. Department of the Interior. Retrieved from https://www.nps.gov/redw/index.htm

National Park Service. (n.d.). *Mount Rainier National Park*. U.S. Department of the Interior. Retrieved from https://www.nps.gov/mora/index.htm

National Park Service. (n.d.). *Olympic National Park*. U.S. Department of the Interior. Retrieved from https://www.nps.gov/olym/index.htm

National Park Service. (n.d.). *Crater Lake National Park*. U.S. Department of the Interior. Retrieved from https://www.nps.gov/crla/index.htm

National Park Service. (n.d.). *Haleakalā National Park*. U.S. Department of the Interior. Retrieved from https://www.nps.gov/hale/index.htm

National Park Service. (n.d.). *Hawai'i Volcanoes National Park*. U.S. Department of the Interior. Retrieved from https://www.nps.gov/havo/index.htm

Brockman, C. F. (2020). *A Traveler's Guide to the National Parks of the Pacific Region*. Falcon Guides.

Muir, J. (2003). *My First Summer in the Sierra*. Houghton Mifflin Harcourt. (Original work published 1911) – Insight into the landscapes of Yosemite National Park.

Sierra Club. (2021). *Exploring California's National Parks: A Complete Guide*. Sierra Club Books.

National Geographic. (2022). *Guide to the National Parks of the United States* (9th ed.). National Geographic Society.

Pope, D. (2019). *The Pacific Northwest's Best Hikes: Trails in Oregon, Washington, and Northern California*. Mountaineers Books.

## Online Articles and Journals

Jones, A. & Smith, R. (2023). "Protecting the Redwoods: Conservation Efforts in Northern California." *Journal of Environmental Management*, 12(3), 145-158.

Miller, S. (2021, May 5). "Stargazing in Joshua Tree: Best Locations and Tips." *Outdoor Magazine*. Retrieved from https://www.outdoormagazine.com/joshua-tree-stargazing

Williams, T. (2022, July 15). "Discovering the Hidden Valleys of Olympic National Park." *Backpacker Magazine*. Retrieved from https://www.backpacker.com/olympic-hidden-valleys

# About the Author and Upcoming Projects

Everett Wilder, a passionate advocate for the outdoors, is a dedicated family man who believes in passing down a deep appreciation for nature to his children. With each visit to a national park, he instills in them the importance of preserving these beautiful places, not just for today but for future generations. He's on a mission to highlight the splendor and serenity found within the nation's natural wonders, showing how these landscapes can shape the values of respect, stewardship, and wonder for all who experience them.

In this book, Everett focuses on the breathtaking national parks of the Pacific Region, aiming to share not only the sights but also the stories and the quiet, awe-inspiring moments that make each park a treasure. As he explores each region, his writing blends historical insights, interesting facts, Awe inspiring sights, Hidden Gems, and mysterious sights and sounds all with a sense of adventure, bringing readers along for the journey.

Everett's journey is far from over. He has plans for additional books in this series, each focusing on a different region of the country. Upcoming titles will take readers from the lush forests of the Southeast to the rugged peaks of the Rocky Mountains, and across the vast, open prairies of the Great Plains. With each new volume, Everett hopes to deepen readers' appreciation for the diverse beauty of America's national parks and inspire them to become advocates for conservation.

These future books promise the same rich storytelling and vivid descriptions, celebrating the unique landscapes and ecosystems that define each region. Everett's goal is to create a comprehensive series that serves as both a tribute to the parks and a guide for fellow adventurers. He hopes to inspire readers to lace up their boots, grab a map, and experience the joy of discovery firsthand, just as he does with his own family.

Made in the USA
Las Vegas, NV
26 November 2024

12676175R00098